THE
TIME
GATHERERS

Writings From Prison

with comments by
GERTRUDE KATZ

Introduction by
HUGH MacLENNAN

THE TIME GATHERERS

Writings From Prison

with comments by
GERTRUDE KATZ

Introduction by
HUGH MacLENNAN

 HARVEST HOUSE, MONTREAL

THE TIME GATHERERS

Copyright © Canada by Harvest House Ltd.
First Edition — December 1970.
SBN No. 88772 — 113 — 3 (paper).
All rights reserved
Library of Congress Catalog Card No. 70-143613
Deposited according to law
in the Bibliothèque Nationale du Québec,
4th quarter, 1970.
For information address Harvest House Ltd.,
1364 Greene Ave., Montreal 215, Quebec, Canada
Printed and bound in Canada

The author and publisher gratefully acknowledge the grants from the Canada Council which have helped to make this publication possible.

All names used in *The Time Gatherers* are pen-names, except for David Read. Personal correspondence is reprinted with permission of the men involved and is acknowledged with thanks.

Proceeds from the sale of this book will go to the Creative Awards Association.

Comments made by Gertrude Katz are not necessarily the opinion of other contributors to this volume.

"For the credit of virtue
it must be admitted that the
greatest evils which befall
mankind are caused by their
crimes."

La Rochefoucauld

Introduction

This book, well called *The Time Gatherers*, is worth the attention of anyone who is conscious, however vaguely, of the vast human and economic waste involved in our penal system. Here you will listen to the voices of men who are as much a part of society as we are ourselves, and who are living proofs of one of society's major failures.

Let nobody think I am being sentimental about men who have been sent to the penitentiary. Some are in the direct tradition of Cain; others of Jacob, history's most celebrated confidence man. Others have been as reckless as Esau and others again as luckless as Ham. Few of those who have done house jobs or holdups did so for genuine economic reasons, no matter what they may say. Egotism, love of excitement, animal aggression, the desire to shine — these very human qualities have very frequently got these men where they are.

Nor is this book an attack on the men who manage penitentiaries. They are public servants with a task more unenviable than that of a modern university president. The system they administer is the system society offers them. If its rehabilitation program is such a notorious failure that Canada has one of the highest recidivist rates in the world, then it is our own selfish affair to acquire some notion of why this has happened.

Our penal system — does this sound startling ? — is psychologically worse than the callous European transportations of two hundred years ago. It is worse than the reviled practice of sending convicted men to Siberia in the Russia of the Czars. Many a transported Highlander or Irishman, faced with the challenge of beginning penniless in the North American wilderness, came through superbly. Dostoievsky did not enjoy his sentence to Siberia, but had he been sentenced to a modern North American penitentiary the chances would have been very slim that the world would have inherited *Crime and Punishment* and *The Brothers Karamazov*.

The inmate of a Canadian penitentiary spends an average of eighteen hours out of every twenty-four alone in a cell that is seldom larger than nine feet by five. His every instinct is frustrated. But why should this concern a well-meaning society taught by romantic behaviourists that human beings have no instincts and are entirely the products of that abstraction called "the environment" ? The emotional and mental tensions caused by frustration of instinct become so intolerable that many a prisoner screams in the night or cuts his wrists — and if he does the latter he is punished by withdrawal of his "privileges" because suicide is against the law. Society, as one prisoner has written, never peers into these ghettos where men slink in fear of one another and in terror of what wells up within their own souls. Society never tries to understand why the men who emerge from penitentiary so often seek to get even. And when a prisoner finally does serve his time and pays his debt to society, he is feared as men always are feared by their fellows when their fellows smell in them the stench of a failure they know instinctively is also their own. While these men are in penitentiary they are ashamed — ashamed of being in prison, they say. But unconsciously they are also ashamed because the human instinct of survival, built into them by an evolutionary process millions of years old, whispers that so long as they are behind bars doing no useful work, almost literally doing nothing, bored beyond the capacity of words to utter their boredom, they are wasting the creative spark without which a human being turns with claws upon his neighbours, or like the wounded hyena devours with relish his own entrails.

Gertrude Katz, who compiled this book and wrote some of it, is no more sentimental about the inmates of penitentiaries than they are themselves. How could she be, after working with them for more than two years? I asked her why she does work which is so exhausting to the spirit when she herself is happily married with children? She told me that her only purpose was to help men who wished to write to do so as well as possible. But first she had to win their confidence. This was especially difficult in the super-maximum security penitentiary which is so flawlessly modern in its design and arrangement that it could serve as a caricature of technological man's success in employing cold reason to produce a scientifically calculated insanity.

Of course Gertrude Katz did not tell me why she does this kind of work. She has no words to say why because they would sound pretentious if she uttered them herself. So perhaps I may utter them for her. She happens to be one of those people who have always existed and always will, who are prompted by something deep within them to pick up the pieces after a disaster.

Being myself a writer, I have long ago learned that it is impossible to persuade anyone to change his attitudes by telling him to change them. Conrad was right when he said that the writer's task is to make you hear, to make you feel, above all to make you see. If other readers are like myself, they will find some pages here which will make them see some things they never saw before.

I hope that this will be the first of many anthologies of work written by men in penitentiaries *while they still are there*. Who am I to make literary criticisms of these writings? They are genuine, of that no doubt. They are the voices of men who have had limited formal education. And one (in the first section of the book) I may tell you, is the personal record of a man whose experience was so similar in two vital parts of his life to William Faulkner's character Joe Christmas that the resemblance is uncanny. The writer of this piece, I am almost sure, never heard of *Light in August*, which is one of the supreme tragedies of the most agonizing of all human predicaments — the literal ignorance of one's own indentity. Because this man was able so truthfully to write some of this terrible pain out of himself, the chances are better than good that when he returns to society his fate will be far different from that of Faulkner's most sombre and tragic hero.

Hugh MacLennan

Preface

While countries hold knives to each other's throats; while atrocities, modern and classical, are used in warfare for the love of peace and Western society debauches itself with sex and pot for a piece of love, it seems almost natural that the human song comes from locked-up men in a penitentiary. They're not always songs of love; songs of loneliness. There are missiles of curses, choked frustrations, anger — and the useless futility born in men who are unproductive and have, instead of a name, a number. A number society stamps like a final judgment on their record... invisible handcuffs for which every one of us has the key.

So prison society becomes a sub-society with a distinctive social ladder, in essence, opposing societies' mores, but reflecting the standards of power respected by world governments. The criminal, who in past performance had the power and ingenuity, dexterity and daring to "pull off a job", is the social leader. If he murdered in the act, he's first class — feared and respected.

"Rapos" and sex-deviates are the untouchables. Not treated separately as mental cases, ostracized and boycotted by the men, they're thrown into the main stream, sometimes isolated by the administration for their own protection.

These are the two main poles of social distinction.

During my two years of work with prisoners who wanted to try their hand at "writing", I did not meet a stereotyped convict as portrayed in the movies or on television. They have as diversified personalities as people you'd meet in any circle, but with a much higher average of individualism. They're not afraid to express their feelings honestly — it wouldn't lower their esteem in their neighbour's eyes, so without the hypocrisy of double-standards their voices are as genuine as the most honest and reckless of modern writers.

Although intellect and craft are understandably uneven, I've chosen the broadest representation of writings. None of these men ever attempted writing before. I had to edit their work, but took great care not to disfigure the contents. The last word was always the author's.

Several days ago, I received a letter from an inmate with whom I had been working for the past six months, trying to manoeuvre him out of a headlock so he could understand and write the poetry he wanted to. In his letter, he unknowingly described how I and possibly some of the men felt when I first entered the prison : *"like a ton of bricks a thought occurred to me. I took a look at myself from your view. If I frighten you then please don't be. I feel miserable* just thinking of the possibility. I realize you have a purpose and if you are frightened of me then you must be a very brave lady to face such a miserable experience as you have these past few months in order to gain a foothold into a world where you believe you can do some good — ... well, no matter. I'll manage to live with whatever ugliness I have till I can change it. Please relax, nothing can harm you with an s.o.b. like me protecting your interests." I never did think he was ugly, or an s.o.b. And on my original visit to the prison I wasn't frightened. I was terrified.

The feeling lasted throughout my hollow echoed walk on cement floors through cement corridors — guards unlocking grated, heavy steel doors in front and behind me. When I left the men that night, fear, pretension, preconceived images dissolved in a stream of guilt — that I could walk out that night and they couldn't.

Thinking rationally now, of course they were there for a reason. They had committed crimes. Society must be protected from law-breakers. I wouldn't like to be held up, mugged, etc. But what is it in the make-up of our society that breeds criminals? Was I, a member of society, guilty of their progression to crime? Did I ever refuse an ex-con a job? Could I imagine inviting an ex-con to my dinner table? Was I jointly responsible for the high recidivist rate by closing the doors to their re-entry into accepted society? ... Some men spoke about "trying to make it out there". I also questioned myself about the loveless institutions many of these men come from — orphanages, reformatories; I wondered about our abortion laws, and babies yet to be born for institutions.

At the present time I only have questions; not even the men knew the answers. Some are trying to find them in their writing.

My thanks to everyone who contributed in any way to the success of this venture. Hugh MacLennan, Irving Layton, and Kay Lines each deserve particular mention, and I especially want to thank my husband, Carl, for his patience and encouragement.

Gertrude Katz

Montreal, Quebec

ONE

And The Walls Came Tumbling Down

Getting used to a medium security prison for me was a simple trick of the imagination. I pretended prison-guards were bus-line inspectors. Electronic steel doors were operated by an invisible Ali Baba, and I was a ghostly foreign agent for Robin Hood.

Once inside the library, the only brutality I faced was honesty; with myself and with the men. My only fear, that I might accidentally don a mask.

The atmosphere in the medium security prison is very relaxed. Still, there are specific rules to follow, and the men are very anxious to know what the rules are for every occasion, every undertaking. Having played the game of "cops and robbers" outside, they want to know the regulations inside, so they can be certain as to when they're conforming or not conforming. When a man would ask me for writing rules, I'd reply there was no set prescription as far as I was concerned — "Write what you honestly feel. If it's genuine, we'll work from there."

I didn't give a writing course. I sat in on a lecture series being given by someone else and let it travel through their excellent grapevine that I was available to help anyone who wanted to write.

Janos Horvath was introduced to me by an inmate who I was already working with on a novel. I had great difficulty understanding what Janos had to say as he was a comparatively new immigrant. After a dozen words I gave up on the disjointed English phrases and tried to read his face. I found myself stranded on a tight formation of barren rock. Finally, in the slow spaced words one uses to the uncomprehending, I asked him to show me what he had written. His face cracked wide open and from the chasm came a torrent of explanations as sheet after sheet of poems mounted on the desk. I'd struck a gold-mine! Amazed, I assured myself with a brief glance that this work was written in English. Gathering up all his material I told him it would have my special attention.

Next morning I read Janos' poetry. There was one poem titled "Composed on Jacques Cartier Bridge" — it rang a familiar bell. I reached for an anthology of poems in my bookcase and turned to "Composed Upon Westminster Bridge" by William Wordsworth. With very little change — just enough to apply the contents to Montreal, lines were identical. I began to laugh. I turned to another titled "Flow Gently Sweet St. Lawrence" and became furious. Like a hound-dog I traced every last poem to its original author. I recall he included "The Judge That Signed the Paper Felled a Man" (taken from "The Hand That Signed the Paper Felled a City" by Dylan Thomas).

The following week I felt like a prosecuting attorney confronting the criminal with evidence. Armed with anthologies, English and American, classical and modern (at least he could have used one anthology to make it easier for me), I went through the poems with him one by one. He listened politely without interruption. At the end of my tirade a confused smile spread over his face. "Me too great writer, like in books ... all have same ideas, use same words." "Janos", I controlled my voice, "you know you took your poems out of these books. Lets forget all about it." He shook his head — "No, no — me, I wrote..." Exasperated, I excused myself.

Janos haunted me after that. He could put more words into a half-pause of conversation than any drain could proportionately accept water. There was no end to what he wanted to tell me. I was told he was attending an English class and I hoped in time we could communicate.

Driving home from prison one night, I began to feel guilty about my impatience with Janos. I projected myself in his position — imagined living in a prison of language within a prison.

A few days later I reached a friend of mine who spoke Janos' mother-tongue and made arrangements to bring her out for a visit. The administration permitted us a private office. As Janos conversed in his native tongue, the tense creases on his face faded. With an interpreter present his explanations were intelligible. He had little means with which to communicate. He could read English better than he could speak it. Borrowing someone else's words to express his own feelings was a compliment to whoever first wrote them. It sounded quite logical.

"But", I explained, "perhaps you have something entirely original to say and can express it with your own words from your own feelings and personal experience. Wouldn't it be far more exciting and satisfying to know the words you put together were your own rather than second-hand ideas?"

He digested this thoughtfully. I remembered his taste in plagiarized poetry was rather good.

Suggesting that he use a dictionary and write about what he was most familiar with, I promised to help make his work legible.

As time passed and his English improved, he did manage to express himself well enough for me to help him produce the following work with an economy of correction. He began with a short autobiography.

"It was an uncertain November; misty, foggy, damp and cold. It was a sad November. For me and a million others there had been bloodshed and tears. How many tears when you find your birthplace obliterated — washed away like dust — debris in the gutter.

"What a morbid fear one can have to find his sleep broken by a rattle on the door... in terror make haste for urgent flight through the window — the door is useless — — utterly dangerous.

"A semi-dark alley... then I tread my way through a cropfield... into a forest that led me far from Hungary, my birthplace home... my family... those I loved, and have loved ever since.

"Leaving my people behind, not knowing where I would end... run... run... or be jailed without hope of seeing them... this way, maybe, some day...

"A minute's walk to freedom — a minute's walk to success, a minute from home, and then to a strange land — strange people... a new home.

"All of a sudden ra-ta-ta ra-ta-ta — a few around me fell mortally wounded or dead. The rest ran — me with them. I ran till I found the inside of my clothes damp and cold... at the same time I heard the sound

of a church-bell nearby — it was the hour of noon.
Putting my hand inside to dry my wet body, I drew
out a handful of blood, jelly-like... then I knew
nothing more."

Janos told me he read magazines and newspapers
in the library; that he understood the Canadian way
of life.

The hand of justice is too damn long.
Power for the poor far too weak.
You cannot make justice meet you half-way
Neither can you make justice to your liking.
But if you realize it then you cease to worry.
Why worry to start with?

There is no justice for the poor
   only for the rich.
The rich grease the palm quick
   while the poor go hungry.
And this is supposed to be modern and an
   efficient justice for all?
Oh, what a cry! What a great disappointment
   for everyone!
Great is the power... great is the crying.

What a strange world to live in today.
Flower power is the thing —
L.S.D. and marijuana and dream long.
To feel and hear strange sensations
   in one broken heart.

To imagine walking on clouds, flying through
   the air.

To smell flowers and hear a million birds
    sing in your ears.
To walk the ever-green at twilight among
    the stars.

I couldn't convince him to title his poems — besides, it really didn't matter.

A crying creature in anguish
Screaming from his deep soul.
After a while the crying in vain
Settles like some inner mass dragged over
A mountain of sharp knives.

The lingering figure behind me —
Unknown to me, but I am concerned.
Those feet burdened and wary
Like iron lids laid over them.

Drops of sweat fall from my face.
A flashing knowledge comes over me.
My heart gives a final thud, then rests a bit.
I turn toward the stalking figure —

And then — then I hear the laboured breathing,
And then our feet move together
Mingling our breath as we walk warily,
Our thoughts slowing down to compare.

Our sorrows in themselves are all too familiar,
Ordinarily I would not have given notice.
But that night, in that moment,
Marked my passage of change.

He told me he came from the countryside — from a respectable home. Before the revolution, he lived on his father's farm.

Through my barred window
I can see trees green;
The scenery is wide and pleasant.
Before me is a field of pasture
And a little hill that limits my sight.

Sadness touches me.
I am within touch of the world —
World that draws my strength
Within my reach — I want to desperately grip.
Within my sight I want to hold.
Within my senses to feel.

Freedom!
Freedom!
Touch me a little.
Touch me gentle.
Freedom, touch my heart and soul.
Freedom! Freedom...

This God-given summer,
Green fields everywhere I look.
This summer has slid into my soul.
This summer has found me unawares.

He tried to find work in Montreal. He did have a job waiting for him when he arrived. The employer was one of his countrymen. Speed was his enemy; automation his rival. Life was very different here — confusing. He was fired.

I am like a lonely hobo
Whose soul is ravished by sorrow,
Silently walking, stopping once in a while
Under some window or in a doorway,
In humiliation turning to beg,
Approaching someone and hoping to get.

At night under blue starry lights,
I walk alone through deserted streets,
Hoping to find something to eat . . .
Something to quench my thirst.
Someone to say a nice thing
Or in passing give blessings to me.
Someone to sing in my ears —
Someone to kiss —
Someone to embrace —
Someone who cares —
Someone who —
Someone.

    He didn't know where to turn. He stole. He stole again, and again.

The first month of the year
Simple were the jail guards.
Not like human monsters
To my convict state of mind.

The judge found fault in me,
Caused to condemn me.
He sent me away in haste
To pay a price of five years.

Now in my third year
It is visible I am beaten.
Frowns have set upon my face,
Gray hairs on my head.

Evenings are dark and lonely.
I hear many sounds of sorrow,
Some piercing and painful
Like someone squeezing his heart.

My heart is dried of blood,
But my laugh will someday be heard –
Because I am the son of man
And such I shall remain.

There was so much in the world he couldn't understand. He questioned.

Who decides the destiny of human population ?
What must one do –
Ask from whom to be a man of wealth.
How must one obtain power
To command world peace.

Power to command flowers to grow rich with scent,
To command them to spread fields with splendour
[of beauty –
Command hearts to open.

Birds, animals, splendour of colour !
Command them to fly, run, dance –
Feel the air with their presence.
Command birds to sing louder

So that the world might hear.
Command them to perch on window-sills
Whistling and singing when people are awake.

To make the earth soft
Not blow away like ashes.
Someone to command all this —
Who ?

They were questions impossible to answer. His thoughts turned to himself.

I

I don't want to be talked about.
I don't want to be praised for my good or bad luck.
I don't want to live my life in excitement.
I want to be my own self.

To walk anywhere people mingle and push —
Hear children shout, run and play.
To give way to older people —
To try and understand the human race.

I like to walk in the rain — in the sunshine.
Like to feel snow on my face melt away.
I like to walk barefoot through morning dew —
Sleep under a tree at sundown.

To walk the streets of city and country —
Walk the road that leads me away,
Then ride over hills, over anything.
Reach my destiny without detour.

II

Darkness and mystery fill my heart.
Approaching thoughts fill me with dread.
I live in the shadow of fear and loneliness –
Life drifting sluggishly forward.

It is the twilight upon the house,
Sun setting long pencils of gold,
Blending gloom and brightness.
Lights and shadows lay asleep.

Determined for the fulfilment of life –
Life that has left me without ties.
An evil system violates the human soul
As years wither all hopes.

I wish to escape the hovering loneliness.
I have been like this before –
Sorrowful and plaintive, scolding and imperative,
When a fetus in my mother's womb.

To me this building is like good prose –
Sober. Free from ornament ; powerful and
Restrained. No flippancy nor artifice about.
A good source of inexhaustible poetry.

In one of his earliest attempts to express himself, he described what he could remember of Montreal and what he missed the most.

Beautiful city is Montreal
Sparkling with a million street lights.
Such a feeling, such excitement within this city –

The exciting go-go-dancers,
The exciting amusement constantly,
The zoo, the amusement parks...
This island is a paradise, a world of her own self.
This city sends me with throbbing heart
Who loves me as I love her.

Night-clubs by the hundreds
Dancing girls by the thousands
The singers singing songs of joy,
Songs of blues, songs of love,
Songs to everyone's heart.

Girls, French ;   girls, English ;
Girls, German ;   girls, Italian ;
Swedish, Spanish, Russian,
Orientals, Indians — just have to ask,
Montreal has them.

The most beautiful French girls
The most exciting English girls
The most hottest Italian girls
The girls of Montreal are the world's
most wonderful, exciting, hottest,
most romantic, most lovable,
the most richest love-givers...

and here I sit in jail...

* * *

The young man who originally paved the way for me to meet Janos was Patrick O'Ree. He appeared preoccupied at our first meeting ; explained he was under sedation — had developed a bad habit of attempting suicide.

Pat told me that after the first time he cut his wrists they sewed him up and threw him in the "hole" (solitary confinement); kept him on bread and water for fourteen days. I asked why? His wry sense of humour took over. "Part of the rehabilitation program. Didn't you know committing suicide is against the law?" He told me the second time he cut his wrists and found himself back in the hole, an administrator got him out and to the psychologist.

Pat wanted to write. He'd made a first try at short stories and wanted my comments. The administration stretched regulations far enough to include me under the formal classification — "Correspondence Course in Creative Writing, uncensored mail". We corresponded in between visits. Here is the first letter I received from him :

Dear Kitty Kat,

Hope to hell this short note finds you and your family in the best of health. You'll have to excuse the writing as I'm as nervous as a reluctant virgin on her wedding night. Am sending along this note of frantic prattle with two mutilated manuscripts. Please overlook the errors in spelling and typing, and please don't suggest I take up knitting.

Pat

My reply in part was :

Just got through reading your manuscripts. You have an amazing social conscience. But the formal manner in which you present the stories coupled with melodramatic adjectives, make them sound like soap-opera bits taken from a Kafka nightmare. If you haven't read Kafka before — don't while in prison.

I returned his work with comments, corrections, suggestions, and wisely stayed away from prison till I received his reaction by mail.

Dear Kitty Kat,

Studied your corrections on both manuscripts and spent the better part of an hour calling you every derogatory name I could think of. Who the hell does this mad woman think she is?

Finally, exhausting myself, I again studied your comments and raced over to the library — dug out a recent edition of the almanac — studied the enlistment requirements for the French Foreign Legion. Luckily, I decided against it ... I get sunstroke easy — uniforms make me nervous. Camels are vulgar animals, they spit and smell.

So I went back to my cell and read my manuscripts again. And you know what? The amount of work that went into correcting this stuff must have been tremendous. I only wish there is some way I can repay you for what you're doing for me.

Please take care —

Pat

Pat's antenna was constantly tuned in for the slightest hint of rejection. He was acutely perceptive and sensitive — had developed a marvellous sense of humour; his self-defence.

In a serious mood, he didn't talk about himself. But he was a wonderful listener, and before long I found myself telling him about my family — my husband and children. One day he showed me a poem he'd written to his young daughter.

Cathy, my dearest Cathy,
if i could only take the stars
from out the heavens
and golden sun from skies of blue,
i would give them all to you, my child.

It would be nothing in comparison
to the pride you gave me
when you missed your toilet
and stood courageously
while blinking through tear-filled eyes
ready to admit your error –
you said, "I'm sorry, daddy".
Or the joy when i came home
and you ran to me – leaped into my arms –
so soft and sweet and pixie with kisses,
fragrant like morning dew on roses –
and said, "I've missed you, daddy".

So now as you sleep, dream my sweet,
of silver knights and flashing swords,
of beautiful queens and devouring dragons.
    i wish you all things blissful –
    for i heard you whisper,
    just as sleep took you away,
        "I love you, daddy".

In the beginning, writing for him was an escape. Reality was what he couldn't escape – found so difficult to accept. On the back of one of his neatly typed letters, I found this written in his own handwriting:

"My house stands on a mountain. The earth is black as the heart of man, brittle and callous as his soul. Sometimes, when the moon is bright, I leave my house, sit on the veranda with the spring breezes blowing and think to myself; what for, what the hell for. Sometimes I stand up and shout — please stop! No need to kill. Take my hand, I love you — love me too. But no one answers me, so I sit down again and think; what for, what the hell for."

He didn't tell me about Cathy's mother. He wrote a poem to her and gave it to me to read.

In this ink black night, as i sit on this bench
and think of things past and present,
contemplating the horror and loneliness of my life,
i see you as a wood nymph
floating down to me on a silver cloud.

You tenderly entwine my hands in yours
and the cloud becomes a mist that whirls about
[you,
but can't hide the exquisite loveliness of yourself.
You take me on your cloud,
whisper a soothing word of courage
and together we swiftly move into the soft velvet
[night.

I remember another night — a soft velvet night,
when you gave me your love...
i slept, only to wake again
in this ink black night —
you were gone.

It's useless to tell a man in prison to watch for the sunrise in the morning. Besides, it's the same sun that set the night before. I could only help him explore the streets in his mind. In a letter, I tried to suggest other dimensions of imprisonment.

At Expo '67, one of the pavilions was called "Man and his Community". One room explored the theme of imprisonment: man imprisoned in his wheelchair; man in his collar (the priest); man by his colour; woman by her babies; the dwarf by his size.

Pat replied with his special brand of satire, giving me a questionable explanation of his heritage.

Did I ever mention my Indian-type blood flowing through these veins of mine that I inherited from renegade Indian-type grandfather? You may have wondered from time to time about my dark complexion. Well, me gonna try and explain the dishonourable happenings.

It all started about hundred years ago on honourable Indian reservation. Grandmother was fullblooded Cherokee. Grandmother married this halfbreed type horse-thief who gave chief of tribe thirty stolen horses in exchange for grandmother who was very pretty-type Indian maiden. But like all heap bad dealings, this story have bad ending, cause both chief and dishonourable grandfather hung as horse-thieves. Poor old grandmother have to leave reservation in disgrace on go-go cart.

She come to Canada where nine moons later grandmother give birth to my ugh-type father who, twenty-five years later, marries pretty-type woman, just off boat from Glasgow, Scotland. She gets tired of him might'tee quick and goes back to homeland.

Me don't remember Scot-type mother. Mus'ta been pretty lady cause look at me, huh ?

After mother-type go back to Scotland, father place me with foster parents who look after me heap pretty good.

I make you honourary Indian maiden if you make me heap member of your tribe. Ha ?

I replied:

Honourable Grand Sonuva Chief Horse-Thief,

Greetings from the land of sour cream and borscht. Twelve tribes of my people (some got lost), welcome you as honourary member. (I just asked Moses, he said 'O.K.')

Gertie

His next letter was hardly in the form of a reply. His moods fluctuated like a precarious see-saw.

Hi Gertie,

Five minutes ago I was lying on my back in bed wondering if I should cut my wrists again. My way of protesting man's inhumanity to man. A minute later I said, nuts to that. I'm gonna write a letter to Gertie — bleed my muse instead. So, if you'll lend me your poet's heart for a moment, I'd like to do some soulful writing.

I wonder, Gert, if man, instead of loving so many 'gods' (spelt with a small 'g') would wake up some morning and say, today I'm gonna try and reach my fellow man. I'm gonna grab him by his coat-collar and say — 'Man I love you. I love you with all the love I give so wrongly to a god I cannot feel nor see nor understand.' As I'm writing this, I'm thinking of saying to the guard when he opens my door – 'Guard, I love you'. I'd better not ... he'd probably put me in the hole for making unnatural advances or something.

But you know, Gert, as I sit here, tears running down my face onto my typewriter, I wonder if instead we were to love one another in the same way we love so mysterious a god, do you suppose there might be no more wars, no hatred, no mistrust? And instead of praying to this god, who, if he is real, is certainly an evil god, we might communicate with each other, with love and understanding – Do you wonder too, when our black, yellow, white and red brothers, now so vastly separated by so many gods, might come together in one family with love as its foundation ... if we might only communicate. Believe me, I'm crying my heart out while I'm writing this and I never felt better.

Pat

Dear Pat,

It would certainly be wonderful if we could all love, trust and respect each other in this best of all possible worlds. And, believe it or not, this is what most people want. It just doesn't always seem that way. People have to battle their own fears of rejection, ego gets in the way – the next thing you know they've convinced themselves 'you're going to hate me anyway, so I'll hate you first'.

I don't believe it's the religious 'gods' that separate the family of man as much as greed, the quest for *power, lack of communication, and a stinginess of the mind in trying to understand.*

Be kind to yourself, Pat. Life offers enough pain independently — ask any person they'll tell you how much they've suffered. Few know how to remember joy.

Gertrude

Pat was desperate to get started on a novel. I suggested he drop the formal tone he used in his short stories and write the way he spoke about situations he was familiar with.

Several days later I received the first six pages of his book; I also received a phone call from the administration. Pat had demanded that an officer lock him and his typewriter up in the "hole" — he needed peace to write his story. He was sent to visit the psychologist who talked him out of it. I was asked for my opinion. "Sounds like a perfectly normal reaction to me", I replied, "perfectly normal".

One of the happy hazards facing a person in my work is that a man could get a parole before he finished a story. At home I found it difficult to suppress my excitement when I received the news — Pat made it! His "ticket" (parole) had come through.

It takes a long time to adapt to society after a stretch in prison. Pat wrote some thirty pages of his novel before his release. He still keeps in touch with me. His book is not yet completed, so in all fairness and respect for his talent, I'll only reproduce a few parts of the beginning of his book.

I, MYSELF

I guess people have always thought me a little rocky... i mean a little crazy. Well, maybe i am. Anyway, my mother must have thought so, or maybe she didn't like the looks of me, because she disappeared from the hospital the day after i was born. Left me alone to face my fate.

Now don't get me wrong, i ain't complaining or nothing. The way i look at things that's the breaks... that's life. You know what i mean.

As for my father... heh! Well, he could'a been any one of a number of gentlemen. You notice i called them gentlemen. I did that cause i'd kinda like to think he was a gentleman.

First of all, before i get too deep into my story, i wanta say that i ain't no goddamned English professor, so you'll just have to excuse my language. Matter of fact i didn't even finish high school. High school! I didn't finish grade school.

Anyway, let me get on with the story. After my old doll leaves me in the hospital, the hospital authorities place me in St. Peter's orphanage for boys.

Oh yeah! Before i forget, i should tell you my name. They call me Ernie – Ernie Blackstone, and i'm writing this story from a prison cell. Now don't get nervous. I didn't kill anybody or anything... just robbed a bank, which i guess is bad enough. I ain't gonna tell you anything about this here prison cause it ain't pertinent to the story. I guess it's enough to say that it's rough in here... rough as hell.

Alright then, i stayed in that orphanage till i was nine years old. I remember very little about my life in that place, cause i guess i was too young to see anything. But i sure remember one day... it was a cold rainy day, and the head Sister calls me up to the front and tells me I'm leaving. I'll never forget that Sister, cause she was always pinching me whenever i came close to her. Anyway, she says to me – "the people are good Christians". Her face gets red when she next says, "they can't have children...". She says this with her nose stuck up in the air like she's sniffing for something evil. And she also says i'm a very lucky young man. Then she takes me by the hand and we leave her office and walk along a hallway that leads into a large room. I can remember that room too, because it was so much nicer than the rest of the orphanage. Furniture looked so nice and new and clean.

There, standing in the middle of the room like they were waiting for a bloody bus or something, were my future foster parents. The man was a big guy, tall, with broad shoulders. I liked him till i looked into his eyes. There was something mean in them. He was looking at me as if he didn't like me either. But i got a good feeling about the woman right away. The only thing was, she looked like a strong wind would blow her over. Long stringy hair hung down below her shoulders. The reason i liked her was because of her eyes. They were kind and lonely. I always look at people's eyes; you can tell a lot about a person from her eyes.

The Sister gives me a pinch and a push and tells me to say hello. So i say "hello". My prospective mother lets escape a long sigh from thin lips and somehow her eyes don't look so lonesome anymore. But my foster father gives a snort and a grunt and says, "Christ, he's skinny!" What he don't know is that i'm a strong kind of skinny — he finds that out later.

— Once, when i was fourteen, i was taken to see this doctor. He put me on a diet to gain weight. After six months of heavy eating and no change in my weight, he told Mrs. Harris to take me to a psychologist cause food wasn't my problem. The nutty headshrinker told her all kinds of funny things about me. One thing he told her is that i got some sort of psychological block, perhaps brought on because i didn't get any love in the orphanage.

You know, for the life of me i can't figure out what he meant. Cause like for the years i'm alive, i spent lots of time in bed with all types of women... had lots of loving... i'm still thin —

Anyway, the Sister says to me. "This is Mr. and Mrs. Harris, Ernie." I say to them. "Please to meet'cha." And stick out my hand.

The guy just stares at my out-stretched hand. He's looking even meaner than before, like maybe i was a smelly skunk or somethin' who dared to stick out his paw for someone to pet.

The room was quiet for a moment, then the woman clears her throat and says. "Hello Ernie. Please call me aunt Julie. You're coming to live with us on our farm — you'll be happy there."

I don't say anything for a moment cause there's something sticking in my throat and i gotta lower my eyes, and that's the first time in my life that i cry, and the last.

The woman says. "Oh dear." She steps forward and puts her arm around my shoulders. "Don't cry, Ernie... everything's going to be fine... there, there."

– She smells of roses and fresh air and her voice is like the sound of a harp... soft and sweet, and this makes me cry all the more. I've never smelt anything as nice as her before. Those crummy Sisters, especially the head one that was always pinching me, smelled like disinfectant and b.o. and cooking starch.

You're wondering how i remember all these things? Well that's another funny thing about me. I never forget. Maybe that's why i'm the way i am... nervous and sensitive.

Anyway, the room is very quiet except for my sniffing, and i'm still standing there with my head resting on my chest... my nose is running, and the tears and stuff from my nose get all mixed up on my chin. The woman takes out a handkerchief from her purse and wipes around my chin.

Suddenly i hear the man say. "Well, we ain't got all day. Lots of work back on the farm... get his mind off crying."

And i hear the Sister say. "Yes, yes. Of course, Mr. Harris... if you'll just step this way we have the release papers all ready for your signature." And they walk towards the office.

When they leave the room, i lift my eyes off my chest and look at the woman. We stare at each other for a long time, and then she says – "What a beautiful child you are. You have very expressive eyes, Ernie. Did you know that?"... i don't answer her, just shift my feet around on the floor. Her face gets red and she looks out into space... i find out later she writes poetry.

The next thing i hear is Mr. Harris saying. "Come on, boy."

As we move towards the orphanage front door, i ask the short and fat Sister who's walking beside me if i can get my things. She tells me that they'll send my stuff in a couple of days because my release was on such short notice the orphanage wasn't prepared. I find out later that they were having a hard time finding a place for me. When the Harris' asked them for someone my age they didn't want to wait around a couple of days to put my stuff together, cause the Harris' might change their minds... so what the hell.

When i get to the door, the Sister calls me back and says. "Here, Ernie, this is for you." She takes this brand new coat from over her arm and helps me into it. It smells of mothballs and everything. First time I've ever had anything new and i almost start bawling again... almost.

And then the Sister does a strange thing. She leans over and kisses me on the cheek a couple of times and says something i don't quite catch. But now that i think about it she probably said – "God protect you, Ernie" – or something like that.

Anyway, Mr. Harris was honking the truck-horn for me, so i turned and ran to the truck, got in, and sat beside Mrs. Harris. As we drove away i glanced back at the doorway of the orphanage. The Sister was standing there, tears streaming down her face. I almost jumped out of the truck i was so surprised! Ah hell, i guess she wasn't as bad as i thought she was.

How do you like that?... Tears running down her fat red cheeks. Still find it hard to believe.

On the ride to my new home, i'd look at Mr. Harris out of the corner of my eye whenever i had the chance. He was a helluva lot older than Aunt Julie... bout fifty, maybe. And stone bald. He sure looked like a mean bugger. You'd think i'd be scared sick of him – only i wasn't. I don't think i ever been scared of anybody.

Now and then i could feel Mrs. Harris studying me. Once she asked me how i felt. I said – "Alright". Only i was lying, cause about that time i began to get a headache.

It got awfully warm in that truck and my skin was beginning to feel clammy.

Aunt Julie says to me. "Ernie, are you sure you feel alright?" And she takes my hand in hers. I can still feel the softness of her touch. And then she feels my forehead.

"Luke, Ernie's burning with fever!"

"Yeah, I'm not surprised. He's a sickly looking thing. Wish I'd had the time to pick a healthy one from that place. Niggers and white trash bastards the scum of the earth. That's all that's in the orphanages these days."

"Luke, please don't talk like that in front of the child." Her hand squeezes mine gently. "I'm sure he'll be alright after a few months on the farm."

"For his sake, he'd better be."

Yup, i think it was on that drive to the farm that i began to hate that old man.

Mr. Harris was a lot older than his wife. Now that i think of it, it was hard to tell aunt Julie's age. She was the kind of a broad, i mean lady, that doesn't show her age. She had a gentle thing about her, like a garden full of blue and yellow tulips on a bright spring day with a playful breeze. Ah hell, she was alright – really swell.

I find out later that she married the old man because her family were poor farmers, and her father owed money to old man Harris. She married him to get him off her father's back. Just like her to do something like that.

When we got to the farmhouse, i really had a fever. I remember Mrs. Harris helping me out of the truck and the bloody house doing a crazy jig. I was sick for two days with a high temperature. Aunt Julie said i kept hollering about the "virgin mary", which doesn't mean what you think, cause the virgin mary is a guy and was a friend of mine in the orphanage.

Old man Harris owned a large farm, and he made me work hard. I had to get up with him at four in the morning and wash them damn cows before he milked them. Do those cows ever stink in the morning. I took to the rest of the farm like a baby to its mother's breast, but it only took me two weeks to hate them dumb cows... except for one cow that i still like.

She was a lazy thing. Always lying around in her muck and smelly manure. One morning we come down to the cowbarn prepared to milk them. Old man Harris tells me to wash off their milkbags, and i wash all the cows till i get down to this one. She's the last one in the line. I take one look at her lying in all her filthy mess, and i say to the old man, under my breath, "up you mister". Then i yell out to him that i'm done. He don't pay no mind because the way we work it, he follows me on down... like when i'm washing the cow's bag he's milking the one i just washed.

Anyway, he must'a thought i cleaned that dirty old cow because he didn't even bother to check her. He just starts right in to pumping on her tits. Well, i guess that old cow didn't like him either. Her tail was all full of crap and green yellowish piss, and she just let him have it, right in the kisser. The tail must'a entered his mouth, and he being so bloody mean must'a tried to bite the tail, cause when the cow brought the tail back the old man's false teeth were fastened right on. You've never seen such a sight like that in your life. You should'a heard the hollering! The old cow mooing away. The old man, all gums – shrieking! What a sight – them teeth swinging back and forth on that poor old cow's tail. A foul-mouthed bastard he was.

I was laughing so hard, i didn't see Harris sneak up on me. I said he was an old man, but that don't mean he wasn't strong. He grabbed me around the throat and choked me until i passed out – but not before i kicked him where he's never been kissed.

When i came to, i was in bed with a broken left arm and a couple of cracked ribs. The old fucker stomped me... my face was so swollen that i couldn't chew food for days, just soup and stuff. I still have a scar on my face to remind me of him. Never did see that old cow again... he must'a let her have it too.

Do you remember me mentioning this friend of mine back at the orphanage, "virgin mary"? His real name was Emile Brossard. His mother placed him in the orphanage. She came to see him once or twice and then stopped coming.

The reason the kids back at the orphanage called him the "virgin mary" was cause he was always praying with them old nuns in the orphanage chapel. Another reason we nicknamed him "virgin mary" was cause he was feminine as all hell — big brown eyes, like a fawn, with long curly eyelashes. And he was fat. So fat that his rump used to sway from side to side when he walked.

But the thing that really gave him away was his high squeaky voice. The first time i saw him was when he was arguing with another kid at the orphanage. I nearly died laughing when he says to this kid, the orphanage bully, "listen dearie, just because your name is Pearl doesn't mean you're cultured, sweetie". Emile had a lot of nerve talking to the bully like that, cause the bully was bigger than both of us put together — but like most bullies he didn't have any guts. When i saw the big jerk was going to take a swing at Emile, i butted in. I only hit him once, and he started bawling his head off.

Emile always hung around me after that. There were other expressions he used, like — "goodness gracious" or he'd say to me — "gee, Ernie, you look grand this morning" — and he'd wave his dainty fat hand in my face. I couldn't get mad at him. Felt sorry for him i guess.

Anyway, i suppose he's a full-grown fag now... walking around out there. That is, if he's out'a the insane asylum they put him in.

He was human, wasn't he? All humans got something to like about them... even, maybe, old man Harris...

* * *

There was no lack of depressives in prison... it was a matter of degree. Then again, who could imagine a "jolly ho ho" while incarcerated. Yet, I had never met anyone who looked as dejected, emaciated and depressed as Leo Munti. Withdrawn, his black eyes brooded in an expressionless face. I seldom heard him speak. He had detached himself from the other men. His crime, according to the laws of this country: "living off the avails of prostitution".

Leo made no attempt to converse with me. I respected his obvious need to be left alone. One day he surprised me by handing me some of his written thoughts.

"I am alone with myself. But then again, am I truly alone? The breeze sings softly into my ears. Surely I am becoming loose upstairs, for didn't the breeze just ask me who I am? Of course, it's only my imagination playing tricks. Anyway, I don't know who or what I am, so how could I possibly answer such a question.

"Man is the strangest of all living creatures. Man discovers what has already been in existence for sixteen or so million years then promptly proceeds to bring about a change. Not always a productive change; merely a change.

"We define and explain the why's and what's of our universe, yet we are unable to prove beyond a theory as to who or what we are.

"In my ignorance, perhaps I will see more, hear more, and learn more of the things I do not know. I will look, listen more closely and turn awareness into my own self.

In my ignorance I must learn to help myself. I must plant my roots firm to weather the decay and ignorance that grows so rapidly in the soil of man."

I didn't feel he expected criticism or comment on his thoughts. It was merely to share a form of meditation.

"In this, my present environment, I find I cannot think in rational, unprejudiced veins. I react to kindness as one starving would react to food advertisements.

"So long as I'm able to say 'tomorrow', feel 'tomorrow' cling to 'tomorrow' — all that is now will not have been in vain.

"Man cannot come out of each experience without carrying some of its dust away with him.

"Because of my situation, I find cynicism and resentment as easy to come by as the lace on my shoes.

"I will grow tall and strong. My wisdom, my faith in mankind will envelop and enfold me.

"No wisdom is greater than the wisdom found beneath the rubble of one's external self."

Looking under the rubble of our so-called North American morality, where does one find more hypocritical attitudes than in sex.

Prostitutes would not exist if there were not men to pay them. Prostitution is a crime. Obviously all males who use prostitutes aid and abet a crime. Therefore, according to law they are criminals. Double standards in sex are a common joke. It's not the men who indulge in prostitutional athletics who are scorned, but the ones caught. The remainder brag. No matter what age prostitute, she wouldn't be in demand without a market. Human attitudes and practices in sex are as numerous as quills on a porcupine It's so easy to rationalize a subjective pleasure. If unable to rationalize successfully, a person makes an appointment with the closest mind-healer and finds out whether or not to feel guilty.

Prostitute-users include the respectable of our society; citizens who vote for law-makers, and I might venture to add, perhaps even law-makers themselves. Why should the "agent" in these dealings of carnal calisthenics take the "rap"?

It's great to moralize and "thou shalt not" — it gives a person a stable sense of decency and an aura of refinement; notice how the eyebrows arch upward towards heaven? Let every man who has ever been with a prostitute in his lifetime turn himself over to the authorities — let's make it on the night of the hockey play-offs (it would save on taxes for renting the large space needed).

Standing above the rubble of conscience, well-dressed self-righteousness points a rigid finger of accusation at one male — the commission agent; the word "whore" is scandalized. As if our respectable and disreputable society breeds no sex diversions and perversions.

I'm not condoning prostitution, nor condemning it. I'm merely puncturing a hole in a venerable hot-air balloon.

Leo was worried that my restructuring of some of his writing into poetry might alter the nature of its content. However, he was pleased with the finished work. The words are his own.

Fortune, come talk with me –
Tell me what future awaits me.
Tell me all there is to know,
That I'm the wisest one –
That heaven waits for me to come.

Fortune, if you can't say all these things
Then listen to the song the falcon sings.
I am no man, merely a falcon.
Black sadness rages within my spirit.

Are you not God ? Are you not woman ?
I go in the direction
Of the forward motions of my body.
My mind goes beyond the reaches of myself.

I am but a figment of the builder's foundation.
There is no way in this environment
To be the person I want to be.
If only I could save my mask for the day of
[hallowe'en.

I touched a hand that vibrated strange tunes
From the strings of my heart.
I turned and fled in anguish.
I am no musician.

Here is the brooding cup of my soul.
Fly with me –

You gazed deep into the valley of my eyes
Saw the volcano that bursts within me.

If it is me you want to look at
You have only to open your eyes.
My world is a jungle.
Its inhabitants a colony of ignorant sado-egotists.

I will walk among them.
I will not walk with them.
Had I the body of the ostrich
I would stick my head in the sand.

Man and not the supernatural is my God.
I will bow to no man, not even myself.
Surely someone will look into my soul,
See the love and beauty growing.

I am not one of many.
I am of all that is black and savage and ancient
And gentle and kind
And all that the people of the earth
Influence me to be. I am many in one.

Perhaps I'm immoral.
Perhaps I'm mad.
Perhaps I'm merely real.

Force will influence me to obey.
Force will never influence me to extinguish my
[spirit.
Man that I am, I have learned to forgive, to forget.
Fool that I sometimes am, I will continue

To seek the hand on the horizon –
A woman's hand.

I saw and asked – "why ?"
I did not see, and asked – "why not ?"

    *   *   *

Jack Hope was an accident. I don't mean an "accident" as if his parents didn't plan his conception. It's just that he was a business accident. He got caught. He was a business man like almost any other business man. The term "business deal" can be used to cover up a multitude of sins, like a woman who wears a turban to cover up a bald head.

Think of middle-class suburbia and your neighbour cutting the back-lawn. That's Jack ! He's the man in the grey flannel suit. The office-manager, salesman. The real-estate agent who knows just what house you can afford. The investment broker who has your best interests at heart. He's your best friend's husband ; your husband's best friend – the one who makes you feel genuinely intelligent and attractive. He's your children's favourite uncle because he has a fun-quality to his laughter. You have confidence in him. His eyes are understanding.

Jack was an excellent public-speaker. I heard him speak to a gathering of men and administration. He looked like a young executive ; earnest and confident. He was articulate and spoke with authority on the subject of a course he was attending.

Because he spoke so well, when the C.B.C. asked me to coach someone to read poetry for a documentary they were making, I asked for Jack. The administration frowned. Jack was not available – he was "incommunicado". The end of his sentence was just around the corner and he'd flipped his lid in anticipation. Tried to smuggle out a note.

Prison buildings and regulations aren't exactly geared for the arty type; a sunburnt turtle-necked and corduroyed director, cameramen dressed to fade into the background, and a stubborn writer who couldn't properly define the word "incommunicado".

I never did ask Jack why he got caught. It couldn't have been serious because his sentence was a short one.

From my experience in the business world, I can think of several persons who might better have been in this state guest-house than Jack. There was one who got a kick out of putting a smaller competitor into bankruptcy. Found it a great amusement. It's no secret that a man can fake bankruptcy, which is against the law, and come out a winner. One man I have in mind made certain that the bankruptcy he pushed a competitor into was only too legitimate. It was no fun doing it to someone who wanted to go bankrupt. And he was a respected member of our society. When his conscience bothered him, I recall, he sent a large donation to a charitable organization. How well he was thought of when his name and sizeable contribution came to the attention of his community!

The film director was asking me whether my work helped to give the men a sense of dignity and self-respect when Jack bounded into the room. He greeted me like a long-waited-for-relative off an in-coming plane.

An officer loaned us an office to rehearse. Jack, relaxed, sat behind his desk perfectly at home. The telephone rang. Jack, unhesitatingly lifted the receiver. "Jack Hope, here – incommunicado!" I can imagine the look on the face at the other end of the receiver. No, he didn't attempt to make any outgoing calls. He respected the trust. But I do remember we both helped ourselves to a candy-mint the officer had left on his desk.

Jack wasn't a prolific writer by a long shot. I kept both of his poems.

AND THIS TOO WILL PASS?

Although clobbered by trouble, grief and woe,
I cling to the philosophical theme.
Some day I'll look back on this, I know,
And laugh till my straight-jacket splits a seam.

MAY

A month, a word
of meaning to
rabbits, birds and bees.

Does it know of me?
    now – May –
    here – May –
if not, why is it
    holding me
    this way
    and letting flowers grow
    in May?

❊   ❊   ❊

If you want to compare "cops and robbers" to the manufacturing business, then "stoolies" are the jobbers. A stool pigeon sells a manufactured criminal to the dealer, or sells out a masquerading dick.

As I'm not in merchandising, I believe the following stories from an inmate, who shall remain anonymous, were given to me purely for their literary value.

YOU GOTTA STAY AHEAD

When Charlie saw the two men and two girls come in the bar, he figured them right away for pete-men. Too slow-moving for stick-ups, too dumb-looking for con-men. Safecrackers alright. The women added up too, fancy and good-looking — but not nervous like when their men carried guns.

Charlie was pleased with himself for this swift classification of four new customers. You gotta be smart to stay ahead and Charlie was always pleased when something served to convince him over and over again that he was smart. Everything was clicking tonight.

Charlie wiped his hands on his apron and stepped out from behind the bar. He walked up to the table and noticed that the women had taken off their coats and draped them carefully over the backs of their chairs making sure the creases were right – the hems not dragging on the floor.

"So far, so good", thought Charlie. "They're going to stay awhile and spend twenty, maybe thirty bucks."

"So what's it gonna be, folks ?" inquired Charlie, with as much friendly animation as his features could express.

The man with the mustache looked at the dark girl and said – "Terry?"

Terry answered. "Daiquiri."

He raised his eyebrows at the little blonde. "The same", she answered.

The man she was with turned to Charlie, gave his own order. "Double Johnnie Walker with ice, no seltzer, no water."

The mustache summed it up. "Two Daiquiris, one rye with water and I guess you heard Joe's order."

Charlie figured the mustache would take the bill. He went behind the bar to mix the drinks. Charlie hadn't learnt much. There must be a hundred guys in the rackets called Joe and neither of the women had even glanced at him. That Terry wasn't worth thinking about anyway, but the little blonde was O.K. Charlie liked a baby face, especially on a small body with good lungs and long red finger nails. Of course, he couldn't tell about the legs, but he'd seen the spike-heeled shoes and that usually meant the legs were O.K. Yeah, the little blonde was O.K. Maybe her name was Lola or Vera.

Charlie crossed the room again, put the tray with the drinks on an adjoining table and before serving them, carefully wiped the bottom of each glass with a cloth. He was taking his time and hoping that the man with the mustache would offer to pay each round instead of piling up a bill.

The "mustache" looked up and asked. "How much, chum?"

"Three twenty-five."

"You own this joint or just work here?"

"Sort of both", Charlie answered with an attempt at a smile. "I manage it for a friend. He don't ever show up, though. Sort of stays in the background. Likes it better there."

Charlie was idly wiping the puddles of water left in the tray with his cloth, but his sharp eye was assessing the fat roll of bills that the man with the mustache had pulled out of his pocket.

The man handed Charlie a ten and said quietly. "Bring another round, chum."

Charlie thought. "'Everything's clicking tonight, alright." That roll must be at least five grand. Maybe more – but certainly not less. Thursday night too. Right for a payroll job. And the time – twelve-thirty. Jesus, it was perfect. They must have pulled the job nice and easy around eleven, ditched the hot car, picked up the girls and walked into the bar. Twelve-thirty. Jesus, it was perfect."

Charlie punched the keys on the cash-register, glanced across the room to make sure he wasn't being watched and slipped the ten into his pocket. He took the change out of the drawer and slammed it shut. Of course, he knew that the numbers on ten dollar bills weren't recorded, but if he couldn't find out any more about Joe and the man with the mustache, at least the ten dollar bill would prove his good faith to the police. You gotta be smart to stay ahead.

Charlie served the second round of drinks and casually said, "Strangers in town ?"

The man with the mustache replied. "Not exactly."

Joe looked up sharply, but before he could say anything, the little blonde chirped. "We might as well be."

Joe turned to her and said. "And what kind of a crack is that supposed to be?"

The little blonde pouted. "Well, I mean... from all the consideration I get from you."

Terry leaned across the table and put her hand on the blonde's arm. "Please, Lola. And you too, Joe. Don't start again. Let's put a dime in the jukebox and dance. This is a celebration, eh Mike?"

The "mustache" nodded but made no move to get up.

"Come on, Joe." The blonde complained. "I wanna dance." Joe wasn't listening. He leaned across the table and whispered to Mike.

Charlie couldn't hear what Joe was saying, so he walked over to the jukebox. "Her name *is* Lola." He thought. "Jesus, is everything ever clicking tonight." Charlie stared at the metallic keys of the jukebox, shoved a dime into the sliding panel and pressed – "How Now, Mrs. Robinson".

Lola got up and walked toward Charlie. Her black satin dress clung like the skin on a grape. Charlie thought her face was like a baby's, but her body sure was grown up. The plunging neckline didn't show much but the breasts were there, full and high – ready to burst out of the dress if she sneezed. That's what he liked. Curves packed with sap and power. "Poison." Thought Charlie. "Poison in satin and nylon."

"Maybe you'll dance with me, big boy? Seeing as my boyfriend over there is not interested."

Even if he didn't want to, Charlie knew he would dance with her. Besides, she was a little drunk and if a smart operator kept his motor running, he could pick up some valuable information. Valuable in real folding money.

"What do you think of a boyfriend who won't dance with you when you ask him to?"

"I wouldn't know."

"Not much help", she giggled. "What's your name, big boy?"

"Charlie."

"Charlie, huh? I had a husband called Charlie, only I called him Churlie."

"Your name's Lola?"

"Yea, I'm Lola. Lola Fazzola, he used to call me... Churlie, that is. But, hey, how did you know?"

"I heard her call you Lola."

"I'm glad you know my name. Sometimes I get so lonesome, Churlie. You'd never, never guess how lonesome Lola gets, Churlie, never."

Charlie tightened his arm around her waist and pressed his fingers one at a time against her ribs. She responded by running her left hand lightly over the hair at the back of his head and pushing her hips forward. "Poison." Thought Charlie. "Mustn't rush things too fast."

The music stopped and Charlie followed Lola back to the table. This was the clincher. If Joe acted sore, then Charlie would go back behind the bar and forget about it. But if Joe didn't seem to mind, then, maybe — a smart operator plays them as they come.

Lola said, "Terry, this is Churlie. You remember Churlie? I mean, his name's Charlie, too."

Joe interrupted. "Bring another round."

When Charlie came back with the drinks, Joe's chair was empty.

"Sit down here, next to me, Churlie." Lola smiled, very friendly-like.

Charlie looked at Mike. Mike didn't offer to pay, so Charlie sat down.

Mike said. "Where'd Joe go to, Lola?"

"I don't know. You know what he's like when he gets sore. I guess he went home, but who cares? I'm sure Churlie doesn't. Do you, Churlie?"

Charlie tried to smile. This wasn't so good. It was up to Mike now.

Mike lifted his glass and nodded to Charlie. Charlie really smiled now and picked up Joe's glass. Charlie was in.

Everything was clicking tonight, alright. If he stuck with them, Lola was almost sure to talk sometime and the police paid for information. Especially if he was right about the payroll angle. He had to be right. Everything added up. But he needed more to go on. The cops wouldn't buy a couple of names like Joe and Mike, even with a ten dollar bill that came from them. He thought of the time Big Red got drunk and insisted on taking everybody over to his place where he pulled a roll out of the piano and stuffed a hundred dollar bill down the front of a girl's dress. The cops had been very grateful for that one and Big Red got ten years.

Charlie announced. "Next round on the house." He stood up and went behind the bar to get the drinks. When he got back and sat down beside Lola, she leaned over intimately with a cigarette between her lips.

"Light me, Churlie, and let's dance some more."

Terry looked at her watch. "It's two o'clock, Lola. Drink up and lets go. It's awfully late."

Lola started to answer but a glance at Terry changed her mind. She turned to Charlie and laid her hand on his thigh. "You come along with us, eh, Churlie? Lola always gets lonesome at two o'clock. Always, always." Now she was running her hand over Charlie's hair, neck and down his back.

Terry rose quickly and took Lola firmly by the shoulder. Mike got up too. "Look Charlie, better lock up and come with us."

Terry opened her mouth, but Mike cut in. "Grab your things, Lola, Charlie's coming with us."

In five minutes Charlie had the bar expertly put to bed. He joined the group at the door with two lit cigarettes in his hand, gave one to Lola, switched off the lights, and taking Lola around the waist, he slammed the door shut.

They crossed the street over to Mike's car. Charlie tried to read the licence plate but couldn't because the others were in the way. He didn't want to make an obvious move. You gotta be smart to stay ahead. Terry got in the front with Mike and as soon as Charlie followed Lola into the back, she began running her hands all over him.

Mike started the motor. Without turning his head, he asked. "You ready to go home, Lola?"

Lola's hand was inside Charlie's shirt. "No, I don't wanna go home. I don't ever wanna see Joe again. I wanna stay with Churlie. Don't I, Churlie?"

Charlie thought fast. That Joe was bad business, so Lola's place was out. He was sure that Terry would suggest another bar and Mike wasn't saying anything, so he took a chance. "Why don't we all go up to my place for a drink?"

Lola answered by whispering "yes" into his ear and followed it with her tongue.

Mike asked. "What's the address, chum?"

Charlie told him and Mike started the car.

The car stopped in front of Charlie's. Terry was the first to get out. She opened the rear door. Lola untangled herself from Charlie so she could get out. Charlie straightened his clothes and took out his keys. He unlocked the front door of the apartment house, held it back against the spring while Terry, Mike and Lola stepped inside. He led them along the hall, up one flight, unlocked his own door and pushed it back to let them in.

Charlie walked through the door and Terry closed it behind him. He switched on the light and started to look at Lola, when Mike said. "Sit down, chum, and don't make any noise."

Charlie's eyes fluttered and his stomach churned while Mike waved him to a chair with an automatic. "I haven't got the money from the bar on me. I always leave it in..."

Mike cut in. "Take it easy, chum. This is no stickup. Terry, go let Joe in."

Charlie sat down and tried to think. Can't jump a cool operator like Mike. Besides, he's keeping well back against the wall. No use yelling. Mike could certainly kill him long before anyone could come. Maybe he could persuade Lola to help.

"Lola..." Mike quickly stopped him. "I said no noise, chum, and no talking."

Charlie kept quiet except for his stomach. It started churning again.

Terry entered the room followed by Joe carrying a long parcel. Without looking at Charlie, Joe started unwrapping it. He carefully unknotted the string and laid it down on the table.

Mike turned to Terry. "Take Lola down and wait in the car. We won't be long."

Joe took the lid off the box, reached inside and walked over to where Charlie sat. Charlie tried to see what was coming, but Joe's foot shot out catching Charlie on the chin. Charlie's head went down, his mouth fell open and suddenly it was full of cotton and Joe was tying the ends of the gag around the back of his head.

Mike laid his automatic on the table next to the box and took out two lengths of clothes line. He tied Charlie's wrists together behind his back and used the second length to pin Charlie's arms securely against his body.

Mike cautioned Joe: "Make sure he can breathe through his nose." Then Mike prodded Charlie with his toe. "On the floor, chum, facing up."

Charlie wriggled out of the chair and eased himself down onto his back. Mike walked over to the box and took out a baseball bat. He hooked one of Charlie's ankles around the leg of the table and spread Charlie's legs apart, using his foot as a lever. Mike beckoned Joe closer. "Sit on his chest."

Then Mike raised the baseball bat above his head and brought it crashing down on the inside of Charlie's knee. Charlie may have screamed or just grunted — you couldn't tell through the cotton.

Joe got off Charlie's chest and Mike pulled Charlie's ankle free from the table. He spread Charlie's legs apart again and brought the bat crashing down on the inside of the other knee.

Mike walked softly into the bathroom, picked up a plastic glass and scooped some water out of the toilet bowl. He came back into the room and dashed the water on Charlie's face. He stared intently for several minutes and watched Charlie's breathing. "O.K., Joe, cut him loose. He's out."

Joe cut through the gag and the clothes-line, pulled the cotton out of Charlie's mouth, picked up the baseball bat and repacked everything in the box. He covered the box with the brown paper and tied it with the string.

"O.K., Mike?"

"O.K., Joe. Let's go."

The two men walked out of the apartment house and over to the car. Both girls were sitting in the back. Mike and Joe got in front. Mike started the motor, then turned around and looked at Terry.

"Next time you go see Big Red, tell him we done like he said."

OPERATION SMOOTHIE

The five of us is manicurin' the lawn opposite the front-gate of the "joint" this morning, when the big door of the "pen" swings open and out comes this hot lookin' dame. She's dark as the queen of spades with plenty of makeup and pale blue shoes with them spike heels so high her chassis wobbles every time she takes a step. She gives us the heavy eye but the screw is right there so we don't say a word. We hold our breath and nobody moves. She goes by on the cement sidewalk, her heels clickin' like little hammers reachin' right into your balls.

Well, she's half way down the long straight stretch that leads to the main highway to town, when the front door swings open again. This time it's a tall good-lookin' guy who's done his time and he's going home. He waves us goodbye and gets into a cab in the front seat next to the driver.

We're watchin' them cruise down the side road that leads to the highway, when, sure enough, the cab comes alongside the dame. The red brake-light on the tail of the cab goes on. Of course, they're too far away for us to hear anything, but we see the dame shake her head "no" and point to the left, away from town. The red light is still on and Ti-Lor, beside me, says – "She'll change her mind cause she knows he's got at least the twenty bucks they give ya when you leave."

We see her shake her head again and point left, but it don't take long and she's floatin' over to the cab and pretty soon she gets in the back seat alone.

So the cab's brake-light goes off and we're all wonderin' which way the cab'll turn when it gets to the highway.

Well, they stop at the corner for traffic. We see the front door open and the guy steps out and climbs in the back.

Ti-Lor says, "Cent pour cent."
Bouboule says, "Champion."

And we all start pushin' our lawn mowers harder than ever as the cab slowly crawls around the corner to the right, headed for town.

* * *

TWO

Labyrinth. Storage For The Human Conscience

Yellow. The walls were painted yellow. Floor rust... like dried stale blood. An isolated visiting room was architectured to one side; rarely used. Only a few of the inmates came from Quebec. A shatterproof glass wall separated the convict from his guest. Voices in the visiting room were monitored by a guard; microphones carried speech.

Ten steps down the long corridor that led into the interior of the Special Correctional Unit, an electronically-operated door of steel bars slid open – slid closed after a person stepped through. There were bars alongside the corridor wall. Bars – as if even the paint had to be secured. Ten more steps down the hall, another steel-barred door slid open — closed. Another ten steps – still another ten steps – the last door slid shut behind.

And music was piped into the huge inner-sanctum rotunda; popular songs, romantic songs, folk songs — "Where Have All the Flowers Gone, Long Time Passing..." Music that soothed, reminded, irritated, till sanity forced ears to block. The circular high – ceilinged room, heavily guarded, resembled the belly of a gigantic octopus with tentacles reaching in all directions — corridors leading to administrative offices and cells.

There was a skylight in each cell... a skylight teased to the ceiling – not for a prisoner to look out, but for a guard to look in, to check his prisoner from the roof. The cell, a concrete and steel vault, measured ten feet nine inches long, six feet seven inches wide. The only opening – a small slot for the prisoner to look into the corridor... into the blank face of another solid steel door.

Referred to by some as a dungeon, this was the super-security penitentiary, officially named the "Special Correctional Unit" or S.C.U. It was built to confine a total of 160 men. (During the year I knew it there were no more than 40 inmates – may the tomb be vacated and remain as a memorial to man's sadistical panic behaviour.)

Solitary confinement in a prison is ironically referred to by some members of the administration as "meditation". It was impossible to discern day from night in a windowless nether hell; an oblique twilight zone for the more sensitive to turn vegetable, suicidal, as the brain was gently pressured to pulp.

An inmate writes:

Alright, I'm stranded and have to make a choice; walk for help or stay and hope I'm found. I decide to walk. But after awhile I have to take the coat off, then other pieces of wearing apparel. Till finally I'm bare. Continuing on because I have gone too far from the original point to turn back... I find the heat is taking control of my senses. Finally I no longer think. I just go on whatever power guides me. The desire to survive has been replaced by the need for shelter. The pores begin to blister like miniature volcanic lava beds... the pain passes through my body till pain controls my entire being. There is no reasoning anymore. Just instinct.

Finally the mind once again makes a feeble effort at taking control, but there is no foundation for it to take hold of, so I think of death, a quick and merciful death. But here again this thought is not rational because I have nothing to kill myself with, and man cannot just lay down and die till after he has passed the point of no return.

Then, as the pain grows to a point of total control, a warmth of a new kind passes throughout the body. This new pain is the pain of realization that my crawling through this wasteland is a walk of death and a joy passes through my frame so that I slow down my crawl, because the urge is to now create as much pain and self-punishment as possible, to purge the soul. Now that death is known, the need to prolong that sense of pure pleasure must be held because then there is time to answer or face all errors of life. So the fingers bite a little harder into the skin to be certain the pain stays... remains as a reminder. Then somehow out of the bleakness a shadow appears...

I'm certain the Canadian government did not construct this building with the intention to drive men insane. It was an architectural experiment for correction. Controversy raged as it was being built. Noted criminal psychologists opposed the plans, bluntly warning that prisoners shut up under such conditions might very well go insane through sensory deprivation – lack of contact with other people and things. They were not listened to.

During the first few months I visited the S.C.U., I heard more rumours of self-inflicted violence than I had heard in a lifetime.

Two stories were oft-times repeated and retold. There was a man who literally starved himself out of his cell and into a hospital where they fed him intravenously to keep him alive. He was returned to the "Special" only to be transferred again. This time to a mental wing.

Another man somehow found the means to slit his wrists. After they were sewn up he was returned to his cell — he pulled the stitches out.

I begged off listening to stories, realizing that people who work under these conditions could develop an immunity to violence or go mad themselves. I preferred doing neither, and exerted my will power to its extreme in order to enter the building, carry out my work, then return home to recuperate. I remember driving home one late afternoon after an exceptionally trying day – unable to shake off the oppression of the day's experience, in a semi-haze I took one wrong turn after another. I remember my panic as night closed in and with what difficulty I finally reached my home. I imagined what it was like for the men inside, and what it would be like for them when they left.

Relations in the S.C.U. between the men and guards were taut. Guards watched the men – watched twenty-four hours a day. The men watched the guards and suspiciously each other. No one was left unaffected. Dehumanization is a subtle process that can slip in like a disease.

How moral is it to gamble with the mental health of human beings ? Tamper with possible existing mental damage? What are the effects of such an atmosphere on a person already mentally ill? Is this building a just and humane answer, or a brutal and efficient way of confining a social problem?

The architecture and program of this institution would make it appear that a man is severely punished for having a problem he could not cope with by himself. The word "correctional" is as misleading as a fraudulent advertisement.

How many ways can one define and apply the word "criminal"? Is it only the law-breaker caught and incarcerated that the term can be applied to, or is every citizen who pays taxes equally responsible for the means an elected government takes to "correct" prisoners? I believe this question came up at the Nuremberg trials. The Special Correctional Unit was built at a cost of two and a half million dollars to taxpayers.

I visited the S.C.U. for six months. Spaced my visits, on the average, to once every two weeks. On each visit I spent from three to six hours on the premises.

*   *   *

My first few meetings with David Read were in the visiting room. As time passed, the administration permitted us the use of an office. We corresponded between visits.

David wrote the following story. He created Stanley, the old man and main character, in a short outline; sent me a copy of his first draft. I edited it, then returned it to him. He went over it, enlarged his ideas at certain points – returned it to me. I edited it again and so it went until finally, he probably felt I did so much work, he wrote my name as co-author.

It took me a while to convince David that the talent it took to create this story was his own. All I did was give it (using his quote) "a haircut and a shave".

MR. STANLEY P. U. SMART

The police cruiser and whining siren came to a jolting stop. A side door was flung open. Stanley could feel uncertain hands trying to be considerate, nevertheless hoisting him out cruelly.

Firmly led past a big sign, peeled paint that still plainly declared to those interested: "Newborn Clinic"... feeling himself propelled on past into a shivering shadowed concrete-like catacomb towards a red globe stating: "Emergency Entrance". Underneath, on a friendless grey steel door, the fine print of a conspirator's contract announced in cheerless dirty white letters: "Psychiatric Admittance". In still finer print: "Leave Guns at Cage No. 1".

Since the archway narrowed at this point, Stanley could feel the closeness, the full bigness of his escorts as they sucked in all the available oxygen. He was left with a funny feeling, as if he could only find their exhale of carbon dioxide for his own collapsing lungs. As though the great slabs of concrete were already falling downwards, inwards, with only seconds remaining before he would be crushed to death. He wanted to scream...

Now the brute holding him firmly on his right reached out an enormous arm – rang a bell. The movement seemed to crush – deprive him of what little life he had left inside his frail body.

The arm repeated the act leaving Stanley numb. All he could hear was a ringing bell somewhere hidden within this giant tomb. The ringing was replaced by the distant sound of keys – steel against steel – changing into a sound of hollow deathlike marching feet. The words "Psychiatric Admittance" disappeared with an explosive ssswish.

In its place stood two beady cobra eyes. Stanley almost wet his pants he was that frightened. He could actually see the flat strike-poised head and imagined the grotesque slimy limb that must lie waiting to strike.

"Yeah!" A muffled voice yelled.

"Police!" The burly brute on his left replied, as though the uniform needed explaining.

"Hey Charley!" The voice inside screamed to someone hidden. "The police", he advised, "with a live one."

Stanley could hear the scuffling of many feet and thought a line was being formed behind that ugly steel door. He trembled with the picture his mind conjured. His two tormentors would fling him forward. Whips for sure – probably sticks and clubs too.

Why did they bring him here? All he wanted was his money and to go home. But they said he had to have a name. Well, his name was Stanley Smart. Before they took it away he had a cheque to prove it. But now, no cheque... no name... nothing. He was no one. Just a silly old man. His thoughts broke as the steel door swung silently inward.

They led him in. A group of starched white uniforms made way for the officers and their sagging burden. Helped into a chair, opening his eyes, he saw white teeth flashing as they leaned over him from all sides.

Through an opening in their ranks he could see the cells... at least the first few. The rest disappeared from his view. In the first cell, through the bars, he could see a pair of bare feet draped by white drawers – hairy legs – a white porcelain bowl. A man squatted; knobbly-kneed, bare-chested, grinning face. Stanley's nostrils twitched... others must have been affected. A voice near Stanley hollered out. "For Christ's sake, Peter!"

Peter mumbled. "It must have been the beans..."

Starched whiteness broke into one livid red patch. Laughter broke Stanley's tension somewhat.

A hand rammed the last of a donut into a mouth. A few held cups and saucers in a professional poise. Obviously, a coffee-break had been interrupted.

Stanley's nervousness waned a little. He thought of his captors as friendly undertakers.

"What's his name?" A voice seemed to shriek, slurred slightly by a half donut which disappeared in gluttonous satisfaction. The mouthful disposed on its way to becoming fertilizer, the question was repeated. "What's his name?"

"What's my name?"... Stanley thought. A tear trickled from his eye. "I don't know." He whispered.

Not satisfied, the voice now generalized to the room at large.

"What's his name? Anyone know his name?"

Stanley could hear the officers explaining about the cheque. Finally, the voice came back to him. "Is your name Stanley Smart?"

Stanley nodded his head. He didn't know what to say. He just nodded his head and wondered how all this started...

* * *

"A name... Stanley reasoned. "Everyone wants a name. Afraid to do anything without a name. Name... identity. As if I was never born. Well I was born. At least I thought I was. Identity... bah!

"... But every now and again someone wants a name. I'm not sure anymore. I have to have some material evidence because people are such simple-minded fools. Having a need, an obvious stress, requires prompt attention. Identity! Vital as the question of survival. I've lived in my present conditional crisis as Stanley Smart for seventy years."

Evidence had never bothered him. Now he wanted his pension so he needed evidence. But there was no proof. The whole world he was born in taken for granted... gone. He was slowly starving.

At the pension office with his incompleted form, biting his nails — not only from nerves... hunger.

"Name?"

"Stanley Smart."

"Well, Mr. Smart, where were you born?"

The questions droned on. Finally. "Alright, Mr. Smart, your story is interesting. What evidence do you have? No birth certificate, eh? Well! Your case will go before a nine-man panel. We will notify you in due course. Meanwhile, because of your circumstances, these suggestions: fish instead of meat, lots of water, crackers instead of bread. – Don't throw old newspapers away. Although poverty is not exactly new to you, you will be surprised how well you can manage, if you're willing to try."

"Is there any choice, sir?"

Stanley went home to wait.

* * *

Leaving the comfortable world of identifiables behind, he walked off the carpeted world of security into reality ... off the pavement and onto the cinder base of Sesspool* Road.

Sesspool Road wasn't exactly what you'd call a postman's paradise. No Sunday sightseers came to travel its tortuous coil. In fact, to reach Sesspool Road, one must leave the world of make-believe behind. Leave the comfortable world of identity, walk off the carpeted universe of material security, pass through traders' stalls of perverse dreams, where, for an ounce of pride, a man's ideals can be bartered for fresh, frozen, or preserved foods at the market place. Down off the pavement begins the cinder foundation of Sesspool Road.

Once here, the first discovery. Sesspool Road isn't a road at all. More like a lane of man's conscience ignored for a lifetime. A lane that leaves well-fed shoppers behind as it wends its way across the many web-like arteries that make up the shunting graveyard of box-cars waiting impatiently for a friendly nudge – a bump that would signal they had not been forgotten.

* Author's spelling. It signifies that the road is not entirely a cesspool, but has something of the cleanness of the sea connected with it.

[74]

Crossing the last set of tracks that form the steel maze of twisted rail-beds, a traveller frantically looks at his feet to see where they are each time the rushing whistle of an engine is heard.

With a shifting curve, Sesspool Road then tries to race past the abattoirs with their stinking stench – the scarlet Buchenwald of modern society – cattle pens with bawling cows in bewilderment, not understanding why green pastures are gone. Next, a row of pink noses pressed tightly between whitewashed slats, waiting for a scratch on the head or a hand to lick – a long line of woolly bleats – "blaa's" – only then does the traveller notice there is no phone for last-minute commutations.

A slight dip at this point runs through several puddles, patches of overflow from the sewage disposal plant that digests the waste of a city. Here, a fine spray-like mist rises. An unpleasant odorous reminder of how man smelled before soap, or after a doctor's scalpel exposed his intestines.

Sloping upward, the roadbed becomes shadowed by the presence, along each side, of cardboard or scrapwood dwellings, called home by many. Here a social distinction is immediately recognized by dwellings made from flattened galvanized tin cans forming rows of rusty shacks.

Still winding, Sesspool Road clears the last shadow, exposing the full expanse of the city's dump. A luxurious plaza for thousands of circling gulls playing the game of competitive society – with a swooping plunge, their victorious cries for a "find". Living proof that judgment is final.

Cutting sharply, Sesspool Road centres itself, carries on through the dump with its scattered stooped bodies covered by shawls, picking what man no longer lays claim to. Lurching across a washed-out gully, it begins to form a peninsula – sticking its tongue out to sea, past more rows of flattened tin homes with unwashed laughing children screaming delight at having such a wonderful can to kick around – barefoot.

Sesspool Road then flexes its way out onto the slithering peninsula. Losing its way here and there, it finally dips down over the surface of a slimy slope that acknowledges the wet garbage dumping area. At the bottom, flattening out, it snakes its way between black lakes of waste oil from "Sesspool Refinery" which happily lays claim to siring this twisting coil of a passage.

Ending in an abrupt butt of weeds, dribbling into a seldom used path, it weaves past an overlooked post with a worn sign: "Zero Sesspool Cres., Mr. Stanley P.U. Smart, Esq., Foreward Ho!" Through tall weeds, piles of long forgotten waste that once prompted man's mind to save, the eyes record from a final knoll the frothy floating turbulent surf crashing desperately against jagged pinnacles of rock. A small tormented frightened house stands alone on its shore; broken with age, decayed with history, dead of memories... the boisterous yell of a robust sailor long silent.

This is where old Stanley lived at seventy years of age, in a long forgotten corner of man's mind. The only visitors, boys with old running shoes gripping the eroded surface of history. They hurled stones through the air in an imaginary effort to sink warships of yesterday, skipping from one battle deck to the other.

In the world of reality, only an old dusty document in some mysterious massive steel vault could establish the fact that old Stanley was a trespasser.

            *   *   *

Sitting on his stoop, as he did every day, Stanley felt better than he had since his waiting vigil for the postman had begun some seven months ago.

His first new discovery, now that he'd been forced to innovate, was tar – an old childhood secret rediscovered. He found chewing the luxurious black Russian gum helped to hold down his hunger. He started searching around that old, almost forgotten world of childhood mysteries to see what else he could find that would force the bowels to move, believing that as long as he could squat once a day he was physically fit. If in doing so, he could make a dandelion happy, he was physically healthy, therefore would live to see tomorrow.

Finished with his work, a recipe of boiled newsprint over an open fire in the middle of the livingroom – the warmth of greedy flaming tongues penetrating his spine — Stanley sat on the stoop and picked up a magazine he'd found on his trapline earlier that morning. Noting its musty smell and soggy condition, he'd take care in turning the pages before it was dry. This was a real prize! If he was careful, read only so much – perhaps two pages each day, it would be like going to the opera, a different concert every night for at least a whole month.

Should he eat now or wait?

Turning carefully to the index page, hopeful of finding something of interest to keep his mind off food, his eyes caught the blaring print: "Why Do People Steal?" by Joe Shluberger.

With an agonizing grunt, he thought. Here he was living on seagull under glass – fifty dollars a plate if caught by the inspector spying from the dump with binoculars, almost starving to death because he didn't have an official name – an identity with which to enter the sacred hall of fame – "Old Age". No birth certificate. Sixteen years of identity on a police blotter wasn't good enough for a pension. Now here was someone in a magazine willing to pay – pay cash to know why boys fail. Any damn fool should know why a boy grows into a thief.

Although... thinking about it, he wasn't so sure. Someone once coined a phrase, "the word is mightier than the sword". He played with both words, then decided the "word" was not mightier than the "sword" for both were thoughts. A word could create its own destruction, but the sole reality of the phrase was in the mis-spelt word. Take away the "s", one word was no mightier than the other.

Coming erect – standing poised, magazine extended before him like a lecturer with his notes, he called out to his empty world – "Good morning, ladies!"

He waited as if for applause, then hearing the flapping wings of two startled monstrous gulls, he felt better... acknowledgement is always gratifying.

Continuing, he spoke with a steady, calm voice.

"Ladies! Mothers! I have been invited to speak to you here in the gracious home of our lovely hostess, on a subject dear to your concerned minds — Why do children reject? The reason I have chosen to speak is so obvious, I'm prompted to ask my own question — why do cows give milk?"

He paused, waiting for at least a polite giggle. All he could hear was the warning horn of a freighter some distance away. The sound somehow reminded him of the moo of a cow. Ignoring the interruption, insult to his pride, he continued.

"What makes a criminal is best told by a case history, so I'll speak from the personal.

"When I was a boy, each time I was naughty Mom would scream, 'You'll end up in prison one of these days!' Then she would cry. 'Oh, how I sacrificed to give you everything.' This was supposed to strike my sense of decency. 'Your father', she continued, 'went to work in his running shoes — ate a cheese sandwich — a radish every day, so you could have shoes with laces.'

"I would have liked to have asked Mom what Dad used for heartburn, but that would have called for a cauliflower ear, so I just withdrew the humorous thought, muttering to myself, sure... without laces I'd have had no shoes... lost somewhere in a boy's unknown world.

"After many escapades... one too many, Mom, desperate, looked for professional advice from a headshrinker who was loonier than a nut-cake himself and titled his own maladjustments: "Child care through the teens". I was twelve, so I'd graduated to teen world a year earlier. Psychology entered the scene.

"Dad was told to treat me like a man. He really thought I was a smart-alec punk, but Mom paid twenty-five dollars for advice. Since Mom loved me, to guarantee full cooperation from Dad, she had to lessen her willingness during the next few weeks to recognize my strutting dance of the cock. Dad's worried. I'm becoming an oversized menace to his foremost concern – himself. But he was going to try – twenty-five dollars worth – since he loved me when I didn't remind him of his own shortcomings.

"He tried a lecture. 'Son, there are two of everything — now I knew Dad was going to make a mess of this reluctant speech, facts he assumed were facts only he had a right to enjoy. The mere thought of his son growing, wanting – needing... made him sick to his stomach.

"I was afraid to hurt him by saying – 'Gee Dad, are you talking about what you and Mom do when she says, close the door, or – not tonight?' I remember his voice asking me what I knew about the birds and bees. I shifted from one foot to the other, hands in pockets. I replied... 'Nuthin'. Dad would never understand I knew too damn much.

"He continued... my mind raced on... I shifted around hoping his words would stop. They finally did. He left me to let his wisdom sink in. Actually, he was glad to get away. I wanted to call him back. The way he spoke of it no wonder he was unhappy. Even at twelve I knew he needed help... either that or I'd better take another look at the birds, bees and Mr. and Mrs. Saunder from our garage roof.

"'After Dad left I remember him telling Mom it was O.K. He'd spoken to me.

"At twelve I was getting too big for swats from Mom, so the 'we'll treat him like a man' helped her a bit.

"After a perfect month from her point of view, one evening I charged into the house. 'Son.' She called. 'Wash up dear, you're late. Dad's home, already at the table.' I blurt out, 'I ain't hungry.' —

"Crash! 'What do you mean, you're not hungry?' Both screamed together, Mom spinned — Dad rose to face me. They shrieked in duet. 'Where did you eat?'

"Somewhat unsure, I replied... I didn't. Meanwhile they could see the peanut brittle caught in my teeth, a mustache of partly rubbed off chocolate, a dab of mustard on my shirt — which proved I was not prejudiced, liking a variety of things. 'Alright!' They shouted. Dad was in no mood after twelve years to be wrong. 'Turn your pockets out!' So with pixie innocence I did. I was clean. The booty well hidden. At least what was left of it.

"With no more incriminating evidence, supper was forgotten. The rostrum lugged out. Professionally prepared booklets on child care already memorized, were delivered like an oracle... I listened...

"Mind you, this philosophy, the family that misses supper together, eats together, if they don't starve together, might have its wisdom, but in this case it took several airings. By the fourth time around, the emotional tones, the entire delivery was much better. I had to give them credit. It wasn't their fault they were about twelve years too late.

"The memorized booklet, chapter 10, section 7, paragraph 9, subsection 4-e, was titled: "Flattery Through Ego". Mom having had more time, takes it from the top. 'Dear, you could be anything you put your mind to being'... (pause)...

"Mom thinks a minute's silence will help the chest expand.

"I want to ask, anything? Afraid to, because I'm uneasy about the whole business. Should I break their hearts? Tell them I know this? That this is exactly what I've been doing for seven years. Being what they didn't want me to be.

"Ha!... I see a look of disbelief on the lovely face of our hostess. I assume, my dear woman, the agency failed to advise you. I am an ex-convict.

"Don't twitch, Mothers. Please relax your purses. I've retired from crime long ago. Now, I'm seventy... too old to care whether there is still something I must avenge. But to help you understand, I'll go back to the beginning."

* *

Lowering the magazine, old Stanley thought awhile. The vision of an audience had withdrawn into the fading shroud of old age. Pondering whether he should go on with this game of charades, seeing himself a total lunatic, he nevertheless continued... spat out... "Mary had a little Lamb!" Involuntarily his whole frame stiffened.

Repeating the five words, with a ferocious oath he shrieked – "Stupidity!" Exhausted he flopped down on the stoop, his anger still with him. He looked out to sea, seeing the errors of yesteryears.

Long ago, on a Mother's lap... she held his head snuggled close, his mouth searching through a gingham dress as she lovingly whispered soft words to brush away his fears and tears.

Just then a movement caught old Stanley's eye. One of those winged monsters waddled close. Old Stanley began to drool, picturing the featherless brute in his frying pan. This one was cunning enough to read his mind – take off to the sky. He muttered as he watched the bird fly away. "Ya got more brains in yer web feet, ya sneaky thief, than man has in his whole damn head." His eyes followed the bird's flight. He screamed in rage. "Mary had a little Lamb... ya damn bird!"

Sixteen years in prison minus good conduct time. Anguish – a hobby. Life – a diabolical puzzle. So easy to be a fool till you have to pay...

Returning his thoughts to his lovely imaginary hostess, Stanley's history regressed.

"My first thought", he recalled in perfect clearness, "was in the fetus stage."

Halting to be sure all the Mothers were attentive, seeing the word fetus ring a bell, he continued. "Thinking my Mom had the damnest poor posture, forcing me into positions only Houdini could manoeuvre, I'd have to kick, jump, flip, to escape. Without a word from me, Mom understood everything I wanted. But Mom got fed up with my demands. Spit me out. That's when all the trouble began. Some big goof playing "Masked Marvel", afraid to unveil himself for fear I'd grow up with a fixation for retaliation, held me upside down by my ankles. He gave me a sucker shot – right hook from way out in left field. I had to use all my will power not to talk... I screamed! Mom thought I was a moron because I didn't speak six languages within the first sixty seconds of life.

"I spoke to Mom throughout the fetus stage. Mom understood then. Now she failed to understand the vital importance of me being able to record in my own limited way what she was doing. A baby can be an adult's vehicle for revenge.

"I had a brain. I came with that much built in. It told me the shortest road to love and peace was to play Mom's silly games. As an infant I had to learn to do "in Rome – as the Romans do". If Mom had studied her history better, she'd have known the Romans in greatness were failures. Average parents are too blind to understand, so Mom raised a failure. Instead of teaching facts, Mom taught fantasy.

"I bet you can't tell me what Mom taught me after goo-goo changed to mama. Go ahead, guess!" Stanley hesitated, searching the anxious faces of his imaginary Mothers, looking for signs of guilt. He threw it at them, imagining they all hated him anyway.

"I knew you'd flunk out! Well, I learnt – hang onto your bloomers, ladies... my Mom taught me... 'Mary had a little Lamb'.

"Now, can you imagine anything so stupid? To teach a boy that! Would Ripley pay through the nose for a line like that or not?

"Oh, so you think I'm stupid, because it means Mary had a little lamb like Jack London had a little wolf. *You* know that! But does a child? A boy growing will always find Jack and a wolf – but can he find Mary's lamb?

"Then Mom taught me Humpty Dumpty... Oh, yes! Lets not forget Alice in Wonderland!

"As I grew, I thought Mary *had* a lamb... Humpty Dumpty was an egg that *could* talk. I even went along with the boogeyman. Then when I had good old Santa laid on me I thought I knew everything. By four I began to worry myself sick that the obese slob would crush my loot coming down our chimney, not realizing till I was five, we had no chimney... just a drain-pipe from the toilet into the apartment above.

"Being a truth-seeker, I believed. Evidence : the cookies, kisses, hugs and applause all convinced me I was headed for greatness. I needed facts, so I hung onto the hem of my encyclopedia... good old Mom... toddling after her, assimilating every sound. Hold out a home-made chocolate-chip cookie to me, I could recite Mom's encyclopedia backwards.

"What reality was I equipped with for school at the age of five, to have someone teach me Mom had been fooling me ?

"Ha! I see it's seeping in. You're right for once in your lives. Some of the most brilliant underdeveloped brains in the world are rotting in prisons.

"The reality I had at the age of five was the hand-me-down cowardly fears man hides behind so he can forget he's controlled by a "Machiavellian Prince". My parents didn't have the guts to let a son grow into a man.

"Love for horses trapped me. Mom helped me become reliant on the big wonderful world of fairyland where I rode a white stallion to success. The dragon was no problem, nor the princess. I just pretended the princess was a cookie. I ate her. Now that she was safely put away, there was no dragon. So I went through life looking for cookies to eat. By five I mastered that world. I needed it as much as the years in prison I served because of it.

"A boy follows what to him is real. With each shattering disillusionment there is a new to follow. The worn-out encyclopedia grows less valuable, the applause diminishes, cookies grow scarcer. Cookies were tangible, so I swiped them till the original reality was destroyed.

"Mary had no lamb. She was just a dumb broad. Somebody probably salted her claim to fame. Humpty Dumpty was the only true story. He was an egg alright – laid by a smarter fool who realized fifty million adults would love him.

"You'd dump *Webster's* for a misprint! By six I'd dumped mine – sought reality in the streets. Equipped as I was, I fell flat on my face.

"Then a goofy teacher thought she was going to help me learn two and two were four. She was in for a shock if she thought I was going to learn another false encyclopedia ... wait to find her out in five more years. I learned Mary had a little lamb another way.

"Now my lovely Mothers, you know why a boy rejected. Wealth might lessen and poverty might increase the chances of rejection, but neither alone creates a criminal.'"

Snapping back to his own momentary reality, Stanley felt strangely better, as if a burden had been lifted. He raised his head. A gull flew by. Too late to duck his head or close his eyes – with a curse he wiped his face and eyes, went inside and wanted to die.

* *

Stanley checked his boiling newsprint. He readied himself to eat when he heard a noise outside. Looking up and out through the space where a door used to be, he saw the postman climb over a bale of barbed wire he had lugged home after it had dropped off a truck. Calling out too late, he saw the postman disappear with a cloud of curses into a trench he knew was some five feet deep — a trench he had dug to let the seepage from the refinery next door run through rather than over his home. Going out to help him, leaving his newsprint gaily bubbling, he saw the postman run several feet down the trench trying to once again take command of his responsibilities which were now floating out to sea on some twenty inches of oil and scum. Stanley hoped, as he watched him make a desperate grab here and there, that he wouldn't lose whatever precious envelope he had for him. Then he noticed the sleeve of the uniformed coat caught on the barbed wire fluttering in the breeze. "Now! If only the postman left that behind, I'd have patches for my pants."

With a feeling of compassion, he walked over to the trench and offered his hand, intending to help. The postman was in no mood for friendship. Clutching his recovered post, he made it to the top without Stanley's help. The letter-carrier stood there, tears rolling down his face, oil slowly seeping from his mailbag. Stanley didn't have the heart to ask him, as a favour, to walk up and down his path until the oil emptied out of his bag. If he would, it would hold the dust down for days. In fact, Stanley was a little reluctant to ask him why he came.

The sad uniformed man handed Stanley a long envelope, black with oil. Having completed his errand, he quickly left by jumping the trench to avoid that hazard and landed squarely on four broken bags of cement Stanley had carefully placed thinking them safe there and out of the way. Stanley shrugged his shoulders while the dusty white cloud grew in size until there was no postman visible any longer.

Turning, he entered his shack. He'd have to remember the sleeve. Left out there too long, a seagull would be off with it. He wiped the soggy envelope as best he could, checking his lunch still bubbling, tore open his official-looking communique careful not to soil the white contents, and pulled out a creamy white sheet. He wiped his fingers several times on his pants and snapped the sheet open from where it had been professionally folded. A slip of paper fluttered out in an arc and calmly settled on the fire alongside his now angry lunch. As Stanley lurched to grab it, it laughingly burst into flames. He had to content himself with reading the beautifully typewritten words which Stanley interpreted —

Your application for pension came up for hearing this day. The votes of the nine-panel members were as follows:

1. *Two members voted you and your references are communists, all disillusioned, looking for a handout. An investigation is being made to check this possibility...*

2. *Two members voted they believed you to be a Martian left behind by a U.F.O. These members believe you're entitled to nothing, should be deported. If their point is well taken, you must, upon proof, return all funds received and surrender for immediate deportation...*

3. *Five members voted your only sin was being born — therefore, qualified as a citizen and a pensioner.*

Enclosed please find your first cheque. Further cheques will follow on the first of each month.

Stanley grabbed his best coal-sack, pulled it over his head through a cut hole, rammed his arms through two other holes not caring that the coal company's name had long faded leaving "pea on me" clearly written across his old shoulders.

He rushed out – down Sesspool Cres., onto Sesspool Road, into the steaming city and the Pension Office. Breathless, he explained to an official what had happened to his cheque.

The civil servant calmly listened, then asked. "May I see your birth certificate?"

Stanley explained and received the familiar reply. "You will have to wait. Your case will be checked ... you will be notified accordingly ..."

So Stanley went home and relit the fire. His lunch was now cold. He thought of the postman and spent a week fixing a bridge over the trench, clearing a path through the wreckage and junk so that the postman would have an obstacle-free course to his empty doorframe.

Each morning found him patiently sitting in his doorway, waiting, chewing a rusty nail, since he felt the iron might help his system.

Finally, one day the air broke with curses. He'd recognize that welcome voice anywhere. Stanley rushed around back where it seemed to originate. He saw no one. Then he noticed a white piece of paper waving in the air near the ground... saw the fingers affixed to it.

"Oh, well... what's the use..." Stanley walked over, plucked the envelope from the hand as the curses continued. The postman stood knee-deep in the hole that was Stanley's out-house. The rage on the postman's face told Stanley this was no time to say good morning, or anything else. Stanley did want to ask whether he would be kind enough to pull the canvas cover out with him. Left in the hole, it was apt to rot. Stanley also passed up asking why the postman came in the back way. Well, no matter...

This was his cheque and he'd cash it now before it could be lost.

At the bank he waited his turn, then proudly pushed the vital life-giving piece of paper through the wicket to be exchanged for coupons that could be traded for almost anything.

Smiling, the young lady looked at the all important document. Glancing his way, she cheerfully asked. "Mr. Stanley P.U. Smart?"

He replied with all the self-assurance of at last having a true indentity. "Yes!"

"Will you please endorse here?" She turned the cheque over, gently sliding it and a pen his way. He wrote his name with all the flourish of a man with status – a man with a name.

The young lady thanked him. Taking his cheque, she stamped it. Now he was ready to receive the absolute proof he was "Smart!" Crisp evidence he was someone.

Then he heard her say – "May I see your identification please?" and a tear trickled from his eye. He wasn't so sure... anymore...

* * *

David Read's poetry was formal prose at first. He learned quickly. He absorbed at a prodigious rate poetry books, my comments, letters, more poems, more books, more letters, critical writings, book reports, questions and questions – I felt as though I was hanging onto a careening ferris wheel that had no brakes.

He accused me of pushing him too hard, that I expected too much. I nearly dropped from exhaustion trying to keep up with him. He wrote more than fifty poems in the space of a few months. It was gratifying to read his thank you note attached to the first group of his collection.

Without you I would not have written. Therefore my work is as much yours as it is mine. However, there were moments when this cell was a sanctuary from your critical eye towards perfection. So I can only conclude that in expecting perfection we shall always fail. But according to your philosophical attitude, in striving for it, we sometimes attain greatness.

"And of course, greatness is determined by history and not by tomorrow. So under your guidance I did the best I could with today, and although I failed to attain in any sense perfection; in accordance with history, I did attain greatness. Therefore, for your pleasure, as you see fit to use it, this is my work.

David Read

THE SILENT KNOWLEDGE

I said "good morning"
she smiled
then I saw her eyes
and cried

I saw an oven
belching into the sky
somehow she still had compassion
understood
why I cried.

TENDERNESS

How can I explain
the dew
that settles
on a petal
without
thinking of the moist
tenderness of a kiss

FEAR

My real fears
unknown enemies are
myselves.

Next come those
beyond self-help –
they smile
and live with revenge.

When I'll go to hell
to help others understand

I'll protect my friends
and loved ones
by not taking them there –
afraid to become a victim
of what I myself create.

What will happen if a smile
proves a mistake?
Will they go quietly away,
or just take a loaf of bread.

VOIDNESS

Walking in voidness
Scattering seeds

Hoping for a harvest
Greater than you or me.

The first sprout – a soul
We call it wavelength

The second – a house
We call it a man

The third – a mind
We call it a beehive

The fourth – a mate
We take it for granted

The fifth – a child
We call it survival

The sixth – a recording
We call it our memories

The seventh – reality
We found it too late ...

OBSCURED BY SUPERSTITION

Silently, I stole in, kneeling to pray,
feeling her presence before the virginal altar,
finding the softness of reality an intertwining
[truth –
we offered it up as a sacrificial rite to the gods.

From the ritual we departed
with the blessing of flesh and blood,
two strangers as one.

SELF - REFLECTION

Mirror, mirror on the wall,
must I lay my tongue down as a bridge
to soften our tread ?

Led by the spark of conflict between us
must we always walk the pavement –
never the clouds or dirt ?

Mirror, mirror on the wall,
must we remain strangers
in a common goal ?

What orbit should we follow ?
I swear to follow, even if
we walk among the dead.

A TRAGEDY

I strode into my world...
cruised its gutters and rooftops,
disguised as a beggar, hopeful of finding pity –
earning contempt.

I spanned man's Christian conscience
with a web of desire – insisting all meet
my standards of subconscious virtue.
I consciously lived like a pagan.

Distorting reality, finding a monster called
erotic, neurotic retreat, I lived
with the constant reflection of God –
bronze idol of an ambivalent introjection.

Now, mask lacerated, conscience exposed,
tormenting waves crash – subside...
tranquility, peace,
smoothes oceans of emotions.

I hear freedom –
Reality like fresh air vacuums my mind's housing
as they stand over me saying a Requiem,
then they lower me into my grave... Amen.

In one letter David's sense of humour took over, and in a giddy mood he did a take-off on a marriage arrangement, computer-style. I encouraged him to develop it into a very short story.

AGATHA AND HOMER

Homer, hearing the front door open and close, pushes the parsnips back into the oven to brown.

Wiping his hands, he hurries into the living room hopeful of a kiss from his wife Agatha home after a hard day's work.

"Hello darling!" He cries out cheerfully. "Tired? Can I rub your feet, back or something so you'll relax? Here! Just lie down on the sofa and I'll massage your ankles. Oh, well. If you feel that way about it, how about rubbing my feet. No? Perhaps a drink before supper?" He'd put some cyanide in it, but with her iron-clad constitution it would probably cure her cold.

"Hard day, eh? Supper'll be ready in a minute or so. Made your favourite, love. Parsnips with diamond onion rings. Are you sure you wouldn't like me to rub... something?" — Seeing her foot kick out, he stops. "Oh well, if you feel that way about it. — Dammit! Look what you've done! Mommy gave me that pipe. Now it's broken! I know you've had a hard day, but you don't have to come in here so bitchy.

"You walk in as though I do nothing all day. A kiss? Like hell... not you. Not even a hug. Not so much as a 'hi darling'. What's happening to us, dear? You haven't said 'I love you' once since you took five days off to have Susan. And Susan's getting married next month. I work and slave all day long to keep our home together... for what?

"I iron your panties so you'll have a fresh pair to show off — I spend hours ironing exact pleats in your mini-mini skirt. Yet not a word — not a word of affection. All I get from you is — 'Homer! You put too damn much starch in my bras!'

"If you don't love me anymore, say so and I'll pack up and go to father's. Twenty-two years married and it comes to this. Is there someone else?" Hearing the small warning sound on the stove, Homer runs to shut off the oven.

Everyone had three or more children nowadays, but they'd only had one. And then he had to wrestle her down for that. Boy, could the computer have made a mistake?

He had a good mind to call Margaret after supper and go out for the evening. Now, Margaret was a woman! Put a coffee flavoured ice-cream cone within a block of her, you end up with a cup of hot coffee.

Oh well, seeing the parsnips had come out nicely, he turned to put them on the table when the urge to ram them into Agatha's face took hold of him. To squash them in her face would be such a joy. — Aw, hell... it would probably help her complexion.

"Supper's on." He called. "Come and get it, dear!"

Seeing her slump into her chair he wondered whether she planned to eat, go to sleep... or pray?

"Well, dear, how was the office today?" he asked.

"Don't you ever shut up?" she shrieked back.

Homer couldn't stand it any longer. Breaking into tears, he ran to the bedroom. Flinging himself across the bed, kicking his feet in the air, he bawled his eyes out.

He heard Agatha call. "Homer, is there any dessert?"

And so Homer knew the end had come. He began packing. Taking what he needed and what Section Thirty-one Thousand, Nine-Hundred and Seventy-Two of the Separation of Wife and Man Act, without lawful notice, would allow.

He planned on phoning father that the computer *was* wrong...; he was coming home.

* * *

As more men in the Special Correctional Unit became interested in writing, suspicions about me arose. Perhaps I was a spy on the administration's payroll. Perhaps I was a psychologist, incognito, doing underground research work. Maybe an ex-prostitute turned into an intellectual cold-blooded sadist getting kicks from watching men suffer. Or a curious, charitable socialite that visited prisons for a hobby.

Ellwood was no hypocrite. His language was honest and forthright.

GUIDED TOUR

Were you ever
on the east side
of the wrong side
of the track —
where murder
is a hobby
and robbery
in the fact?

The small guy
he'll get busted
thrown in
the damn ole' tank
while the Square John
kneels to glory

and to God
he says his thanks.

    The hooker
walks her turf-way
the heister
robs his bank —
the pusher sells his monkey
and the user wants to crank.

    The fuzz
does walk his paw-trol
as all good po-lice do
and checks
all doors and alleys
'cause
he's a peeper in radiant blue.

    The night life
is real swinging
from twelve till half-past two
especially
in the gaol-yard
where 'Ole Ellis
takes a few.

    Now, you know
about the East side
of the wrong side
of the track
so hop right in your Caddy
and for fuck-sake
don't come back.

STAND FAST YE GALLANT ORATOR

for Irving Layton

"What the hell are you,
young Charley?" I asked —
as he took my hand and squeezed with bulbous
[fingers
as though lost friends we'd been all the while,
enjoying my agony of profound bewilderment —
ague for a master of poems.

Lyrics and sonnets are the ambition
and calling of me. So when I heard
of this flamboyant ding-dally
while in this barren domain.

Had the luck to see him indignant
among the critics who had the guts
to stand alone.

If need be he'd tell us all the truth
of the working perverted brain.
He knew how to relate the torrid tales and acts
that Kings and Saints do love as much
as life with baleful lust to pluck —
   the new born sun.

ALL IS NOT LOST

Earth
emptied its poetry
into the nightmare of dogs
of dying nations

each
an intellectual disgrace.
Every
human face and sea lies
locked in frozen verse
singing
unsuccess in a rapture of distress.
Time
deserts the feeble heart
yet starts the healing fountain
in prisons of our day.
We'll teach the free man yet
to praise his dog
in the death of still another
day.

SELECTED FEW

From among the many
a few of us emerge
who will not be submissive
will not be purged.

We're told we must be grateful
for the blessings bestowed on us,
upon our sinful bodies
to be redeemed from heaven's pus.

    Well daddio, we got news for you,
we like it in the heat –
'cause where in hell on God's green earth
are all us friends to meet.

INDIGNATION

... is the emotional trait
of man's suppression of men,
whose sins of violence rational or not
cause valiant ones to tremble and quake.

Those of sadistic nature
the "jollies" they seem to pop
while stripping men of their moral wrongs
with karate, head-locks and rot.

The "Keeper & Kept" should assimilate
in the eyes of the righteous and pomp;
mutual accord of salvation –
vanquish the whole bloody lot!

Yes indignation is the forte
of the inside men looking out
through rusted bars with swollen eyes –
they chose this life,
    search for the reason why...

MOTHER - BEGONE

From out of the night of the misty cave
where no daylight or comfort dwells,
you weave my dreams of peace or fear
that give perpetual hell.

Wrap your eyes with the hair of day
blind your form in a mantle dark,
seduce the lips with a passionate kiss –
lead, oh witch – show the way.

Teach the lilacs how to grow
touch weary souls with your opiate wand –
open the gates to all my loves
give reason for hopes to flow.

Be near, oh witch, when my light is low
to tickle the heart of the sick –
yet desert me, oh witch, when my health is dry
the blood and the nerves play tricks.

✿   ✿   ✿

    I neither enjoyed nor hated my work. I didn't even feel committed. My attitude was more like the mountain-climber who, bruised, cut and shaken is asked – "Why are you climbing a mountain?" She stupidly replies, knowing few would understand – "Because it is there." My peak of ambition was to give every man who wanted it a key to an open door where he could express his resentments, bitterness and disillusionments; where he could remember his loves and happier moments. My aim was towards the freedom of the mind. I did it for the love of freedom.
    I continued visiting the Special Correctional Unit – spaced my visits to once every two weeks. In the interim, I rebuilt my objective armour.

✿   ✿   ✿

    Ken Nisson was a young man. An unfortunate misunderstanding occurred after a press conference was held at the S.C.U., at which Ken and others were present. Ken told a newspaper reporter, who was obviously ignorant of prisons and prison life, that "This was the best break he ever had" (meaning the Creative Awards Association). The reporter quoted Ken as having said that being transferred to the S.C.U. was one of the best breaks Ken had ever had.

Another newspaper reporting the news conference warped the facts to such an extent as to make it appear that David's writing ability developed from pins stuck into him by the Warden.

Ken had written some lyrics for music. I think he composed the following ones in a prison before being transferred to the S.C.U. He told me, back home he had studied piano; learnt how to accompany himself on the guitar.

THE NIGHT

Night holds a million mysteries
It has a million eyes,
Strange sounds and voices
And many secrets to hide.

There are those who wait for darkness
Before they roam the land
To carry out their evil deeds
Unnoticed by any man.

There are those who find it peaceful
They relax and watch the sky
And find in it a serenity
That makes one unafraid to die.

And as the dawn comes slowly
And the sun lights up the sky

Millions of people wander out
Unaware of the night gone by . . .

Ken titled the next verse with his convict's number. I changed it to 1970.

1970

I wonder what the world would be like
If they told me it's O.K. you can go.
The world would seem empty for me just the
[same
I'm a man with a number not a man with a
[name.

* * *

When a man is released from prison, either on parole or at the end of his sentence he has three strikes against him when he comes out on the street. Having been removed from society for a lengthy period, the psychological re-adaptation to a sort-of-a-freedom of choice and direction is understandably difficult. Finding a means of self-support during this time is obviously formidable enough. But obtaining a job in the shadow of a convict's number, overcoming his own existing fears and public prejudice is quite a tall order. What, really, does society expect him to do? Starve? Lie? Steal? Continue a convict for the rest of his life so that prejudices can be justified?

Meanwhile, back in prison, who draws the line between punishment and correction? It would certainly ease a hypocritical conscience to think of all prisons as "correctional institutions", but using this label to cover up a hopeful truth is only to rationalize a lie. Correction in penal institutions, to a great extent, is on a do-it-yourself plan framed within punishment and questionable rewards of relaxed restrictions. Most of the period in prison is spent just gathering time for release.

Prisons are peppered with a curious lot of rehabilitation "experts". For example, there are the noted professionals like sociologists, psychologists, criminologists – they look down from their gilded cages of learning, and, with textbook patterns before them, juggle "types" into already tabled slots. Clergy of all denominations – each with his personally spiced formulae for salvation and cure faithfully make the rounds (reminiscent of mission impossible). "AA" sponsors weekly club meetings where sober testimonials are encouraged from memory – very much like a starving society forming a gourmet's club — if there's nothing to eat at least it's a place to talk about indigestion. And, there is our organization, Creative Awards, with instructors in the arts who must sometimes appear like refugees from *Alice In Wonderland*'s Mad Hatter tea party.

My first shock regarding the prison population was that approximately 85 per cent were foundlings or had come from broken homes. When a man claimed he was adopted, in most cases he referred to a foster home – parents of other children who could use the extra stipend per month the government allotted. Memories were often dressed to bolster an ego. Rejection – anticipated rejection, was covered with a shield of false bravado that sometimes erupted like a child's tooth hollowed by high fever. The need was not for rehabilitation in all cases. Some men did not have the fortune of circumstances to "habilitate" to begin with.

Prisoners, it is said, are supposed to be anti-social. Today's prisons are supposed to teach and enforce rules and regulations so that offenders are turned into law-abiding, peace-loving citizens. (I wonder how many ex-convicts can attest to this archaic, unrealistic rationale.)

Coleman Wells, a long-time recidivist, wrote his views regarding prison while incarcerated in St. Vincent de Paul Penitentiary (maximum security). His background was classical for the prison obstacle course – orphanage, foster homes, reformatories, and finally, various Canadian penitentiaries. This is the way he sees it from inside the walls:

"Society legislates that it will rehabilitate hell out of you should you stumble into 'Debtor's Yard'. Yet society never peers into these ghettos to probe the productivity of their own getting even. The fact of the matter is, Canadians do not openly admit that prisoner reform is a problem left far behind. I admit we are far better off than we were; I haven't seen a leg-iron in years.

"To a person idly standing by on the sidelines watching the police cruiser ease to a halt in front of the grey-stoned facade of the penitentiary – as he watches the shackled prisoners crawl out and disappear behind the thud of a huge door, he may well assume this to be the end of a social problem. How sadly I disagree. It is when these unfortunate people have, as the saying goes, paid their debt to society and crawl back out that resentment and hostility are about to flourish.

"Is the debt of man's injustices really paid by his serving a prison sentence, or is it terminated only when the reverend gentleman sprinkles a handful of dirt over the gaping hole and wistfully whispers, 'ashes to ashes... dust to dust?' Are ex-convicts given consideration as fellow human beings when they seek employment to coincide with society's demands and to support themselves and their families, or does the conceived myth of a "criminal" form an image that crumbles his usefulness and ability as a fellow citizen.

"To be forced into the social atmosphere of a penitentiary is probably one of man's greatest fears. But then again, he is not aware of the total degradation unless he has been subjected to it at one time or another in his life. To slip quietly back into the mainstream of today's confused society is an even more frightening experience for some. Frightening to such an extent that some would commit a crime in order to be caught and returned to an atmosphere that has become more familiar. Unfortunately, while imprisoned, they have endured such mental torment that only time can tell if they can ever revert to the norm.

"When dealing with people, human beings, we are not always dealing with creatures of logic; human emotions are involved. To venture into the convict's world it must be understood that they are first human beings and must be understood as emotional individuals with emotional problems – not just so many digits that compose a number.

"To attack the core of prison problems, a tremendous effort must be applied to understanding convicts as they endure an environment utterly replete with tension, boredom, harassment and degradation ; a life completely devoid of changing routines, encouragement or interest.

"Anxieties, largely unknown or understood by many penitentiary inmates are cultivated to a degree by fear of their own thwarted heterosexual impulses. When anxiety is suffered to an intense degree it completely interferes with the normal tenor of existence. This is compounded in prison, because the environment to begin with is of an abnormal origin. Many inmates suffer from acute depression. To escape this state of mind they regress from reality. In certain cases and during this period or state of repression, the individuals not only are vulnerable, but sometimes seek homosexual companionship in an effort to release this build-up of pressure. Fatigue and loneliness breed nothing but fear ; fear leads to resentment, resentment to rebellion, and the cycle eventually revolves to more serious crimes and longer prison sentences.

"Power of thought, inherent in humans, is so constructive, I fail to understand why it has been so much neglected. No one has yet seemed to realize the human resources and potential capabilities of convicts. There is only one way I know of to ever get another person to do anything : to create the desire within a person to want to do it.

'A logical assumption' — you say.

"Nevertheless, for the lack or want of understanding it has been completely overlooked.

"It is more than easy to find fault with politicians of today, and for that matter, yesterday and times before us. Instead, I will simply ask you, Mr. Citizen :

who is it that advocates our government's policies for prisons, conditions, rehabilitation programs and the like? Its you Mr. Citizen, who would rather look the other way at the mere mention of this so-called correctional apparatus.

"No, I am not excluding myself from guilt or responsibility. As a matter of fact, sitting hunched over my machine pecking out this article, I'm acutely aware. Simply by the sounds and strains of this alien world I am constantly reminded of the debt I must pay for my lawlessness. Drift in here for a moment and listen. Mingled amongst the continuous chains of conversation are a few verbal chess games in progress — numbered moves are being yelled out. Every minute a toilet flushes. Throughout the evening the sound of gushing water is a part of the convict's world. It's heard, tolerated and forced out of the mind. The chatter of a typewriter drums out a beat. An argument over a hockey game between a guy on the third tier, and another on the second landing is being baited by those listening with nothing else to interest them. This night is the same as last night, the night before, and it would seem all the tomorrows. Under deadlock in a maximum security penitentiary, punishment is inflicted daily and nightly by the grizzly nothingness of its environment.

"Men from all walks of life are herded together in these penitentiaries. For some, floundering helplessly on the sharp rocks of reality, they require treatment of the mind to overcome their immaturities. Punishment by the establishment is merely forcing these unfortunate individuals to regress further and further away from reality – the reality of themselves.

"Every now and then it is reported in the newspapers that such and such an institution will be constructed for x number of dollars. Your dollars! However, the locations of such prisons and penitentiaries are far removed from hospital and university facilities of our metropolitan centres. Prisons should be located near cities and universities where communication with and assistance from industries and educators can be established. Such facilities would offer research, treatment and training so essential to rehabilitation.

"It should be remembered that to conform to society's ideals a person must be a part of that society. Prison-furlough plans should be implemented, inmates should be permitted to maintain family ties and attach themselves to part-time jobs outside which would contribute to the welfare and gainful support of their families. Within the prisons themselves, improved industry-type employment is desperately needed to combat the monotonous fatigue of useless and non-productive jobs that grind the initiative out of a man and do nothing more than pass time.

"I hear so often reference being made to the hard-core criminal. Is there such a person? If so, he constitutes no more than five per-cent of any prison's population. Such people do exist. But they are not hard-core (according to myth) criminals. They are mentally sick individuals who require psychiatric treatment. To segregate them from other inmates, to salvage the salvageable, is a sensible attitude. But to punish these sick individuals who have been segregated for lack of knowing what else to do with them is a barbaric and insane attitude and an impossible approach to ever correcting their mental disorders. A swift execution to alleviate their suffering would be less expensive and a great deal more humane.

"An apostle of art once said: 'Ultimately, the bond of all companionship, whether in marriage or in friendship, is conversation.' It is very necessary for convicted criminals to establish a dialogue with people on the outside during their incarceration. Isolation from society speaks for itself."

Printed by L. E. Marquis Ltée, Montmagny, Que.